D0076436

TANNERS OF TAIWAN

Westview Case Studies in Anthropology

Series Editor

EDWARD F. FISCHER
Vanderbilt University

Advisory Board

THEODORE C. BESTOR
Harvard University

ROBERT H. LAVENDA
Saint Cloud State University

Tecpán Guatemala: A Modern Maya Town in Global and Local Context
Edward F. Fischer (Vanderbilt University) and Carol Hendrickson (Marlboro College)

Daughters of Tunis: Women, Family, and Networks in a Muslim City
Paula Holmes-Eber (University of Washington)

Fulbe Voices: Marriage, Islam, and Medicine in Northern Cameroon
Helen A. Regis (Louisiana State University)

Magical Writing in Salasaca: Literacy and Power in Highland Ecuador
Peter Wogan (Willamette University)

The Lao: Gender, Power, and Livelihood
Carol Ireson-Doolittle (Willamette University) and Geraldine Moreno-Black (University of Oregon)

Namoluk Beyond the Reef: The Transformation of a Micronesian Community
Mac Marshall (University of Iowa)

From Mukogodo to Maasai: Ethnicity and Cultural Change in Kenya
Lee Cronk (Rutgers University)

Black Skins, French Voices: Caribbean Ethnicity and Activism in Urban France
David Beriss (University of New Orleans)

The Iraqw of Tanzania: Negotiating Rural Development
Katherine A. Snyder (Queens College, City University of New York)

Tanners of Taiwan: Life Strategies and National Culture
Scott Simon (University of Ottawa)

Forthcoming

Urban China: Private Lives and Public Culture
William Jankowiak (University of Nevada, Las Vegas)

Muslim Youth: Tensions and Transitions in Tajikistan
Colette Harris (Virginia Tech University)

TANNERS OF TAIWAN

Life Strategies and National Culture

SCOTT SIMON
University of Ottawa

A Member of the Perseus Books Group

All rights reserved. Printed in the United States of America. No part of this publication may be reproduced or transmitted in any form or by any means, electronic or mechanical, including photocopy, recording, or any information storage and retrieval system, without permission in writing from the publisher.

Copyright © 2005 by Westview Press

Published in the United States of America by Westview Press, A Member of the Perseus Books Group.

Find us on the world wide web at www.westviewpress.com.

Westview Press books are available at special discounts for bulk purchases in the United States by corporations, institutions, and other organizations. For more information, please contact the Special Markets Department at the Perseus Books Group, 11 Cambridge Center, Cambridge, MA 02142, or call (617) 252-5298 or (800) 255-1514, or email special.markets@perseusbooks.com.

A Cataloging-in-Publication data record for this book is available from the Library of Congress.
ISBN 0-8133-4193-0 (pbk.)

The paper used in this publication meets the requirements of the American National Standard for Permanence of Paper for Printed Library Materials Z39.48-1984.

10   9   8   7   6   5   4   3   2   1

For Kai, who inspires me and fills my life with music.

Contents

Series Editor Preface

One of the values of anthropology is that it deals with the mundane as well as the exotic and spectacular. Indeed, rendering the mundane extraordinary and the spectacular mundane is what makes cultural anthropology compelling, shaking up our received sensibilities and helping us look at the world in different ways. Work is generally considered to be of the mundane—all the more so in the alienated world of late capitalist production. In this book, however, Scott Simon shows how economic production is intimately tied to the formation of national identity.

Tanners of Taiwan focuses on workers and managers in leather tanning factories in southern Taiwan. Simon uses this small industry of family firms with its artisanal heritage as a microcosm for understanding Taiwanese national identity in an age of globalization. Simon takes on several key theoretical issues in the social sciences today, most boldly conceptions of hegemony, resistance, and identity. He reveals the complex circumstances under which individual and national identities are manufactured alongside the leather uppers that may find their way into Texas boots.

Taiwan is a unique place. For a generation of anthropologists it served as a synecdoche for Chinese society, but Simon and other young scholars question this presumption. The degree to which Taiwan is culturally "Chinese" or is something unique ("Taiwanese") may seem like a mute issue to students of globalization's dynamics, but it is a concern very much at work in daily life and national discourse on this island of 36,000 square miles. The Chinese did not arrive until the seventeenth century, on the heels of Dutch colonization, and most were male migrants who married aboriginal women. Their descendants have come to be known as the "natives" of Taiwan, numerically overwhelming the peoples who first occupied the island 12,000–15,000 years ago. Given its fifty years of colonization (1895–1945), one could say that Taiwan is as much Japanese as Chinese. Nonetheless, national discourse was oriented toward the country's Chinese-ness during the post–World War II rule of the Chinese Nationalist Party led by Chiang Kai-shek (which included forty years of martial law, the longest ever imposed). Under the Nationalists, "native" Taiwanese culture (itself a hybrid of indigenous, Chinese, Dutch, and Japanese influences) was denigrated, while Chinese high culture, with its 5,000 years of history, was celebrated.

Simon's primary focus is on family-controlled tanneries in southern Taiwan. The tanning industry here, first developed under Japanese rule, is shown to be intimately connected to the ebb and flow of the global economy. Taiwanese tanneries flourished in the 1970s, benefiting from an easing of tariff barriers and the subsequent freer trade in skins and tanned hides. We learn that the leather trade is surprisingly global: hides from the United States, Japan, and elsewhere are shipped to Taiwan where they are tanned into leather, and then the leather is shipped to China or the Philippines or elsewhere to be made into baseball gloves, shoes, and other products that often wind up back in the United States. Given this history, one might expect the trade to have benefited from the wave of globalization in the 1990s. Yet, Simon shows how Taiwanese tanneries now have to compete with mainland China's cheap labor. In fact, many successful firms have moved at least some production to China to take advantage of cheap labor and lax pollution regulations. The tanners of Taiwan find themselves in a period of economic upheaval requiring major changes in their forms of productive organization, just as the politics of national identity has come to the fore of public discourse.

Simon describes the traditional importance of kinship ties in family firms and how current circumstances have moved families to hire professional managers. Capitalist markets work best when they are anonymous, when the "distorting" influences of social and family ties are muted. Yet labor relations in Taiwanese tanneries rest on precisely such kinship and social networks. The managers Simon interviews value what they see as a uniquely Taiwanese form of capitalism—the free market with a human face. Here personal connections are key, the "human touch" *(jin-cheng-bi)* a fundamental part of management. There are clear aspects here of patron-client relationships, in which client exploitation is softened through asymmetrical personal bonds. At the same time, the emotional bonds of *kam-cheng* act to decrease social distance between workers and management and ameliorate alienation.

Long a significant employer of women, the tanning industry now employs a growing number of foreigners. Simon shows that there is a sense of class

Photo courtesy of John Monte

Mont's Carpet & Flooring was the 2009 Gloucester County Women's Slo-Pitch Champion for the ninth year in a row. The MVPs were Rose Jones, Lisa Johnson and MaryAnn Guddo. The team was coached by Darryl Errickson and sponsored by John Monte.

ExxonMbl	NY	1.68	2.4	11	69.83 +.26	-12.5
FannieMae	NY	...	...	...	1.68	+121.1
FordM	NY	...	...	...	7.01 +.18	+206.1
FredMac	NY	...	...	...	1.98 -.06	+171.2
FultonFncl	Nasd	.12	1.6	...	7.47 +.02	-22.3
GenElec	NY	.40	2.4	13	17.01 +.25	+5.0
Goodrich	NY	1.00	1.8	10	56.30 +1.37	+52.1
GrtAtlPac	NY	...	...	...	9.03 +.67	+44.0
Heinz	NY	1.68	4.2	14	39.59 -.06	+5.3
HewlettP	NY	.32	.7	15	47.01 +.66	+29.5
iShEMkts	NY	.60	1.5	...	39.28 +.59	+57.3
iShR2K	NY	.83	1.3	...	62.02 +.43	+26.0
Intel	Nasd	.56	2.9	45	19.53 -.01	+33.2
IBM	NY	2.20	1.8	13	121.61 +.04	+44.5
JPMorgCh	NY	.20	.4	54	46.47 +1.92	+49.2

SonyCp	NY	.28	1.0	...	28.37 +.04	+29.7
Solarind	NY	1.19	3.4	10	34.81 -.16	-12.6
SprintNex	NY	...	...	...	4.29 +.04	+134.4
SPDR	NY	2.42	2.3	...	107.07 +.62	+18.7
SPDR Fncl	NY	.38	2.5	...	15.34 +.34	+22.5
Sunoco	NY	1.20	4.3	4	27.93 +.14	-35.7
SusqBc	Nasd	.20	3.2	18	6.34 +.23	-60.2
TorDBk g	NY	2.44	...	...	64.39 +1.32	+82.0
USSteel	NY	.20	.4	16	50.24 +2.22	+35.1
Vale SA	NY	.54	2.3	...	23.28 +1.01	+92.2
ValeroE	NY	.60	2.9	...	20.35 +.21	-6.0
VerizonCm	NY	1.90	6.4	13	29.51 +.02	-12.9
WalMart	NY	1.09	2.1	15	50.99 +.08	-9.0
WellsFargo	NY	.20	.7	38	29.39 +1.10	-3.
Xerox	NY	.17	1.8	18	9.21 -.23	+15.6

Stock Footnotes: g = Dividends and earnings in Canadian dollars. h = Does not meet continued-listing standards. lf = Late filing with SEC. n = New in past 52 weeks. pf = Preferred. rs = Stock has undergone a reverse stock split of at least 50 percent within the past year. rt = Right to buy security at a specified price. s = Stock has split by at least 20 percent within the last year. un = Units. vj = In bankruptcy or receivership. wd = When distributed. wi = When issued. wt = Warrants. **Gainers** and **Losers** must be worth at least $2 to be listed in tables at left. **Most Actives** must be worth at least $1. Volume in hundreds of shares. **Source:** The Associated Press. Sales figures are unofficial.

NYSE Composite	7,047.13	+78.54
Amex Market Value	1,803.54	+17.31
Nasdaq Composite	2,146.30	+8.26
S&P 500	1,071.66	+7.00
S&P MidCap	704.20	+4.54
Wilshire 5000	11,113.95	+80.51
Russell 2000	620.69	+4.72

	8,187.14	4,181.75
	1,944.73	1,130.47
	2,266.45	1,265.52
	1,255.37	666.79
	805.08	397.97
	12,889.41	6,772.29
	751.66	342.59

Currencies

	Last	Pvs Day
Australia	1.1456	1.1588
Britain	1.6352	1.6194
Canada	1.0683	1.0778
Euro	.6760	.6813
Japan	91.24	92.13
Mexico	13.3235	13.3805
Switzerlnd	1.0240	1.0327

British pound expressed in U.S. dollars. All others show dollar in foreign currency.

Money Rates

	Last	Pvs Week
Prime Rate	3.25	3.25
Discount Rate	0.50	0.50
Federal Funds Rate	.00-.25	.00-.25
Treasuries		
3-month	0.10	0.13
6-month	0.20	0.21
5-year	2.42	2.38
10-year	3.45	3.45
30-year	4.21	4.26

Mutual Funds

How to Read the Mutual Fund Tables

Here are the 1,250 biggest mutual funds listed on Nasdaq. Tables show the fund name, sell price or Net Asset Value (NAV) and daily net change, as well as 12-month total return.

Name: Name of mutual fund and family.

NAV: Net asset value.

Chg: Net change in price of NAV.

Total return: Percent change in NAV for the last 12 months, with dividends reinvested.

Footnotes: b = Fee covering market costs is paid from fund assets. d = Deferred sales charge, or redemption fee. f = front load (sales charges). m = Multiple fees are charged. NA = not available. p = previous day's net asset value. s = fund split shares during the week. x = fund paid a distribution during the week.

Name	NAV	NAV chg	12-mo %Rtn
AAL Mutual:			
BondInv	10.44	+.09	-3.2
CoGrp	14.52	+.14	-3.3
MuBd i	10.44	+.09	-3.5

identity that goes along with being a worker, but he argues that this is but one piece in a larger mosaic that includes kinship ties, social identification with one's role in the production process, and national dialogues of collective identity. After martial law was lifted in 1987, organized labor tentatively emerged. But Simon shows that shop-floor forms of indirect resistance (à la James Scott's "weapons of the weak") remain important.

The leitmotif of much current ethnography is the effects of neoliberal reform and economic globalization in the 1980s and 1990s. Simon brings this concern to the small factories of southern Taiwan, showing the complex effects that ensue. Simon also addresses the difficult relations between Taiwan and the People's Republic of China and the way they are being defined and redefined in national political discourse and on the shop floor. This book makes a substantive intellectual contribution to the burgeoning field of the anthropology of work, with a close eye to ethnographic detail. The subject matter is fascinating and should be compelling for students and professionals alike.

This book converges neatly with the Westview Case Studies in Anthropology series' goal of publishing ethnographic texts that clearly situate the population being studied in larger global contexts. The series presents works that recognize the peoples we study as active agents enmeshed in global as well as local systems of politics, economics, and cultural flows. There is a focus on contemporary ways of life, forces of social change, and creative responses to novel situations in addition to the more traditional concerns of classic ethnography. In presenting rich humanistic and social scientific data borne of the dialectic engagement of fieldwork, the books in this series realize the full pedagogical potential of anthropology: imparting to the reader an empathetic understanding of alternative ways of viewing and acting in the world as well as providing a solid basis for critical thought regarding the historically contingent nature of our own cultural knowledge.

Edward F. Fischer
Nashville, Tennessee

Acknowledgments

This book began as my Ph.D. dissertation, which in its original incarnation explored anthropological debates about the relationship between culture and economic development. In that work, I concluded that the structure of specific industries in Taiwan is more productively explained as a product of institutional frameworks created by subsequent political regimes in Taiwan than as a manifestation of Chinese cultural values.

My mentors in Taiwan, who include scholars as well as friends and research participants over a period of five years, pointed out to me that their behavior and values were informed by much more than Confucianism or Chinese culture by any other name. Indeed, their economic and social lives were strongly shaped by the legacy of Japanese colonialism, the terrors of martial law under Chinese Nationalist Party rule, ethnic tensions, a yearning for democracy, and competing nationalist ideologies. Some, but not all, of the people I met insisted that they were not Chinese at all. Many of them perceived public discourses on Chinese culture to be a form of political hegemony brought to Taiwan by a colonial power, and they encouraged me to study issues of ethnicity, nationalism, and identity. Those suggestions led me to political anthropology and the discovery that Taiwan is a perfect case study for many of its central debates.

When I began teaching university classes and presenting public lectures in Ottawa, I soon realized that students and other members of my community knew very little about Taiwan and how it became "Free China." Most had learned about Taiwan through cable news television and other media, sources that depict Taiwan's situation as merely a historical split between the Chinese Nationalist Party and the Chinese Communist Party. Even the more nuanced ethnographies of Taiwan, many written when the country was still under martial law, portrayed Taiwanese social life as primarily a manifestation of Chinese Confucianism. Although I do not deny the scholarly value of those texts, they provide very little background for students wanting to understand why most Taiwanese do not wish to become citizens of China, despite constant pressure from Beijing to do so.

Taking all of this into consideration, I decided to transform my Ph.D. dissertation into an ethnography of working life in Taiwan that focuses on identity, nationalism, and the political dimensions of culture. Writing primarily for undergraduate students, I have tried to keep my theoretical points as clear and simple as possible. I have also related my activities in the field to illustrate how anthropological insight is gained. I hope that this book will serve for many undergraduate students as an introduction to anthropological theory and practice, as well as a tool for learning more about the complex political situation in Taiwan.

Research for this project was supported by a McGill Major Fellowship from McGill University, Montréal, Québec, as well as by a grant from the Wenner-Gren Foundation. The R.O.C. Ministry of Foreign Affairs generously invited me to join a Canadian delegation to observe the 2004 presidential elections. Their investment in my research made this book possible.

As with all anthropological projects, this research would have been impossible without the help of many individuals. Most of all, I would like to thank the tanners of Taiwan, who generously gave me their time, not to mention tea, food, and sometimes even transportation. Mr. Wang Nian-chu of the Taiwan Regional Association of Tanneries also provided me with a directory of tanners, other written materials, his perspectives on the industry, and occasionally a folk song played on the guitar. Other friends in Tainan and Kaohsiung facilitated this research by providing contacts in leather tanneries and often acting as volunteer research assistants. The hospitality of the people of southern Taiwan is without parallel in my work and travel in more than thirty countries. Although I would like to give each of them credit personally, I will refrain from listing names in order to preserve their anonymity. For the same reason, all names of leather tanners in this book are pseudonyms, and identifying details have been modified in the life histories.

I also have a long list of intellectual debts. I am especially indebted to Chuang Ying-chang, who introduced me to the Institute of Ethnology at Academia Sinica and first encouraged me to study Taiwan. Hill Gates and Linda Arrigo drew my attention to questions of class, gender, and ethnicity in Taiwan long before I even arrived in the country. My Ph.D. supervisor, Laurel Bossen, also encouraged me to look at the material dimensions of social life.

After completing the field research for this project, I was granted a postdoctoral fellowship at the Institute of Sociology at Academia Sinica in Taipei. There I learned much more about small Taiwanese firms from Shieh Gwoshyong and Ka Chih-ming and about the complexities of Taiwanese ethnic and national identities from Wang Fu-chang, Chang Mau-kwei, Wu Nai-teh, and other colleagues at the institute. Lu Yu-hsia, who also mentored my subsequent research on women entrepreneurs, enlightened me on the role of wives in the tanneries.

In writing the results of this research, I benefited first from the advice of my thesis committee members—Laurel Bossen, Don Attwood, and Jérôme Rousseau—and then from external examiner Stevan Harrell. As I transformed it into a book, I learned much from the comments of Steve Chen and an anonymous reviewer and received valuable assistance from series editor Ted Fischer, as well as Karl Yambert, Steve Catalano, and Iris Richmond at Westview Press. I thank Jennifer Swearingen for her copy-editing. In addition, members of the transnational Taiwanese community in both Taiwan and Canada inspired my thinking as I wrote. I was particularly inspired by both Taiwanese and Canadians working on grassroots empowerment projects in Taiwan, including Dr. Albert and Sophie Lin, Dr. Ed File, and Donna Loft.

I would also like to thank the members of my family, who endured my absence while I lived in Taiwan for several years. My parents, Dan and Angela Simon, even made the long trip to Tainan to visit me while I conducted research. I also wrote this book with the knowledge that my nieces, Alaina and Julia Keene, would someday be my most avid readers. Te Pit-ngo, Ma Lingming, and Ma So-ing, my family in Tainan, made this book into a project of love. Finally, D. Kai Ma accompanied me on this project from fieldwork to final revisions on the book manuscript. Without their support and encouragement, this project would never have been completed.

Notes on
Transliteration of
Mandarin and Taiwanese

The transliteration of Mandarin and Taiwanese languages presents a difficult problem for all anthropologists working in Taiwan. The transliteration system of hanyu pinyin promoted in the People's Republic of China has become the standard in academic works and thus has the advantage of being easily understood by sinologists. Hanyu pinyin, however, was designed for the transliteration of the Mandarin Chinese spoken in northern China, a language that is as different from Taiwanese as German is from English. Since Mandarin is not the language spoken in the homes and workplaces of many Taiwanese, including the individuals depicted in this book, rendering their words into hanyu pinyin would be as unfaithful to the original field experience as would be writing a book about the Navajo with only English renderings of their native terms. Selecting the appropriate transliteration thus becomes a difficult task of balancing the needs of different readers, including Taiwanese readers who will be interested in this book.

In order to provide the readers with the most authentic sense of Taiwanese social interactions as possible, I use the Taiwanese orthography from Embree's (1984) *Dictionary of Southern Min* to transliterate personal names and native terms, especially when they have been presented to me in Taiwanese by research participants. In order to facilitate typesetting and reading by nonspecialists, however, tone markings have been omitted. The glossary (Appendix I), as well as the English glosses in the text, should make it clear to readers which terms are involved.

In the spirit of presenting Taiwan in its own terms, however, I acknowledge that Taiwanese transliteration is not always the most appropriate choice. Since Mandarin Chinese is the official language used in Taiwan, some research participants used that language to describe their life-worlds to me. For those terms, as well as for place names, I have used the modified Wade-Giles system common in Taiwan and used officially by the post office. For the benefit of scholars looking for works in libraries, I have used hanyu pinyin to translate proper names in the bibliography. Exceptions are made for authors who use other spellings in their publications. In spite of the idiosyncrasy of these choices, I believe it is the best balance between often conflicting goals of facilitating comprehension by non-Taiwanese readers and accurately representing daily life in Taiwan.

Tanners of Taiwan

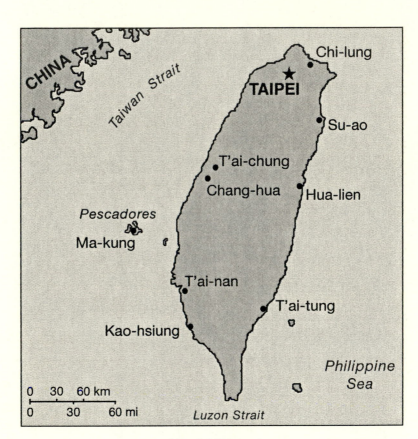

Map 1.1 Taiwan.

CHAPTER ONE

INTRODUCTION

> To realize the potential of Great Taiwan, it is crucial that all people of different historical backgrounds come together, forming a new common background distinct from that of the continent.
> —LEE TENG-HUI, *THE ROAD TO DEMOCRACY*

In March 1996, Taiwan held its first democratic presidential election. The People's Republic of China (PRC) perceived Lee Teng-hui, the incumbent candidate from the Chinese Nationalist Party (Kuomintang, KMT for short), to be a "radical" proponent of Taiwanese independence. Through the media, they warned the Taiwanese voters that tragic consequences would follow if he were re-elected. To underscore their threats with concrete actions, they launched missiles into the harbors off Taiwan. To outside observers, it appeared that war was imminent. Nonetheless, Lee won the election with 54 percent of the popular vote in an election described widely by global media as "the first presidential election in *5,000 years of Chinese history.*" Lee himself, however, did not so enthusiastically embrace a "Chinese" identity.

China perceived correctly that Lee Teng-hui would change Taiwanese society and destabilize its identity. Lee, the first native-born Taiwanese to hold the presidency, brought a different perspective on "Chinese-ness" to Taiwan. Over the course of his presidency, national and ethnic identities became central issues in Taiwanese social and political life (Corcuff 2002a; Katz and Rubinstein 2003; Wachman 1994). As president, Lee Teng-hui angered China several times by, for example, stating publicly that he considered himself to be more Japanese than Chinese and by declaring to the German media that

China and Taiwan are two distinct states with "special state-to-state relations" (Lin and Tedards 2003: 39–40). He even referred to his own party iconoclastically as the "Taiwanese Nationalist Party."

During the Lee Teng-hui era (1988–2000), debates about "Chinese-ness" versus "Taiwan-ness," long suppressed under Chinese Nationalist rule in Taiwan, slowly resurfaced into the mainstream of Taiwanese life. In the 1990s, social scientists began "indigenizing" scholarship, shifting the focus of anthropological and sociological research from Chinese culture to Taiwanese society. At Lee Teng-hui's insistence, school textbooks were revised to focus on Taiwan rather than China, and as a result, debates raged about the introduction of Taiwanese history into the primary and secondary school curriculum. In schools and local history clubs, as well as artistic and literary circles, there was a renaissance of interest in local history and use of the local Taiwanese language in the public arena (Corcuff 2002b). In a context of free media and a thriving civil society, debates about Taiwanese identity flourished at all levels of Taiwanese society. "Indigenization" became a household word.

These were significant changes, especially when one considers that the study of local history and the promotion of Taiwanese language were both once considered as evidence of illegally advocating Taiwanese independence. It was in this context that I moved to Tainan, in the south of Taiwan, to conduct anthropological field research on the leather tanning industry from August 1996 to May 1998.[1] Questions of national and cultural identities marked my entire research experience and subsequent scholarly career, just as they continue to mark a contentious political and social life in Taiwan.

One of my first interviews took me to a leather tannery in Changhua County. I got up at 6:30 A.M., rode the train to Changhua City, changed to a bus that left me at a remote stop on the highway, and walked along a narrow road through rice paddies for more than one hour in the hot sun, asking repeatedly for directions on the way. Even asking directions was challenging, since many people in rural southern Taiwan speak Mandarin Chinese with difficulty, if at all, and I was just beginning to learn Taiwanese. By the time I finally arrived at the tannery, I had already been on the road for five hours. I was exhausted, hot, and thirsty.

Just inside the iron factory gates, two shirtless men were unloading a truck of raw hides. Flies hovered in the air, attracted by the putrid smell of skins and rotting flesh. I was thankful to leave them behind when they pointed me toward a small building designated as the factory office. I walked inside and introduced myself to the young lady working as accountant, secretary, and receptionist. She motioned me to the back room, where three middle-aged men were drinking tea around a small wooden table, and said I should speak with Mr. Chhoa.[2] I stood in the doorway and, to their astonishment, spoke in Mandarin Chinese to explain the purpose of my visit. I asked if it would be possible for me to interview either the owner or his wife for an anthropological study.

Figure 1.1   Leather Tannery, Tainan County.

"What does leather tanning have to do with anthropology?" asked one of the men, presumably Mr. Chhoa.

"Anthropology is the study of culture," I replied. "I am writing my Ph.D. thesis on the relationship between Chinese culture and industrialization. The leather tanning industry makes an interesting case study."

"Then you will have to go to China," he said. "There are no Chinese here."

The three men laughed heartily as he turned his back to me and continued pouring tea. They spoke to each other in Taiwanese, a language then completely incomprehensible to me because it is so different from the Mandarin Chinese I had learned in university. Having come so far, their dismissal of my project was painful. I stepped toward them, desperately hoping to get my task accomplished after such a long and arduous journey.

"I'm sorry," I said. "I meant to say that I am studying the relationship between *Taiwanese* culture and industrialization."

"That's better," said the man. He invited me to sit down. He took a cup from the tray beside him, cleansed it with boiling water, and then poured me a cup of tea. He introduced himself to me as Mr. Chhoa Kok-ui, the owner of the company. He indicated that one of the other men was his production manager and the other a supplier of tanning chemicals. We exchanged name cards.

Turning to me, Mr. Chhoa said, "Actually, we don't like the Chinese here. Have you ever heard of the February 28 Massacre? When the Chinese Nationalist Party came to Taiwan after the war, they killed tens of thousands of

Taiwanese people. Ever since then, they have oppressed us Taiwanese. You should write your thesis about that."

I ended up spending several hours in that tannery and gained the first of what would become one of many impromptu lessons in Taiwanese history. Mr. Chhoa invited me to share lunch with him and his workers, showed me around the tannery, answered my questions about family and firm organization, and gave me unsolicited opinions on both Taiwanese history and contemporary politics. Throughout the afternoon, he stressed that Taiwan is not part of China. He said that Taiwan had been colonized by "Mainlanders" who came to Taiwan with the Chinese Nationalist Party after 1945 (see Chapter 2) and subsequently proceeded to forcefully assimilate the Taiwanese into their own version of Chinese identity.

Drawing broad connections among linguistic, ethnic, and national identity, Mr. Chhoa argued that Taiwanese and Mandarin Chinese are the languages of two distinct peoples who should logically have their own sovereign countries. When he was a school child, he reminisced, his teachers fined students as punishment for speaking their native language of Taiwanese in school. He hoped that with democratization, the Taiwanese would emerge from Mainlander domination and assert their own political identity. The eventual result would be international recognition of an independent Taiwanese republic. Even with democratic reforms, however, he worried that it would prove impossible to completely decolonize Taiwan, since the People's Republic of China is ready to occupy Taiwan militarily if they declare independence.

At the end of the day, Mr. Chhoa drove me back to the bus station and invited me to visit him in the future. He said he was willing to help me because he hoped I would inform the world of Taiwan's difficult situation. "I hope the Americans will help Taiwan," he said. "Taiwan really is pitiful." He was not the only tanner who spent hours with me in order to drive this lesson home, with the hope that I would eventually publish a book on the issue for an American audience.

POWER, IDENTITY, AND NATION:
TAIWAN AS A PARADIGMATIC CASE

As challenging as these experiences initially were, they opened up the possibility of writing a new ethnography on power, identity, and nation in Taiwan. An entire literature, in fact, has evolved around issues of nations as imagined communities (Anderson 1991), culture and power in colonial situations (Comaroff and Comaroff 1992; Wolf 1988), ideologies of domination (Wolf 1999), as well as the relations between culture and memory, power and place (Trouillot 1995; Feld and Basso 1996; Gupta and Ferguson 1997; Lefebvre 1991 [1974]; Pred 1990). These works from anthropology and related disciplines make it clear that nations, cultures, ethnicities, and identities are ongoing processes that exist in a global context of colonialism, state expansion, and class struggle. Since everyone, from President Lee Teng-hui to tanners in rural Taiwan, was challenging received ideas that Taiwan was inherently "Chinese," I realized that Taiwan is a paradigmatic case of contested national identity in a postcolonial situation. It was, however, a heretofore unexplored area of anthropological inquiry.

Two years before I went to Taiwan, Stephen O. Murray and Keelung Hong had already argued that China-centered anthropologists were "looking through Taiwan to see 'traditional' China" (1994: 17). They argued that the Taiwanese under Chinese Nationalist rule were like colonized peoples in South Africa or in the Americas and that the anthropological view of Taiwan as part of Chinese culture only provided further justification to their oppressors. In their opinion, American anthropologists adopted this discourse for a number of reasons, including the loss of researchers' access to China after the Communist Revolution, Chinese Nationalist Party support and facilitation of research that supported their ideological claims over Taiwan, and a general tendency in Western academia to orientalize (Said 1978) non-Western societies as timeless cultural entities rather than as complex societies struggling to find a place for themselves in the contemporary world. Murray and Hong's book, which unfortunately suffered from poor editing and insufficient command of anthropological theory, was dismissed as political polemic for the Taiwanese independence movement and thus had little impact on the anthropology of Taiwan. The critical anthropology of the 1990s and 2000s, however, leads inevitably to a reappraisal of their main argument.

In the 1990s, issues of power, culture, and identity became central to the study of "Chinese" societies, including Taiwan. Arif Dirlik (1997), for example, argued that a discourse of "Chinese capitalism" in Taiwan, North America, and elsewhere suppresses class, gender, and ethnic differentiations among the people encompassed by it. In a similar line of reasoning, Susan Greenhalgh (1994) argued that "Confucianism" in Taiwanese family firms was merely an ideological justification to extract unpaid labor from the women and younger men in the bosses' families.

Attention to questions of power, culture, and identity led some anthropologists in the 2000s to explore local Taiwanese identity as well as Chinese historical and cultural influences on Taiwanese society. Melissa Brown even put identity at the center of *Is Taiwan Chinese?* (2004), a study in which she documented Taiwan's aboriginal past and how it has influenced local identities. Anthropologist Bonnie Adrian similarly wrote, "I intentionally invoke a division between Taiwan and China that regards Taiwan as neither exemplary of China nor reducible to it" (Adrian 2003: 37). *Tanners of Taiwan* adds to that literature by looking at how Taiwanese tanners, as well as other actors in their firms, negotiate different identities in contemporary Taiwan. In the workplace and at home, they craft identities at the same time that they craft leather.[3]

NATIONS AND CULTURAL HEGEMONY

Whether Taiwan should be labeled as "Chinese culture" or "Taiwanese culture" is more than an academic question. As anthropologist Eric Wolf said, "The ability to bestow meanings—to 'name' things, acts, and ideas—is a source of power" (Wolf 1988: 388). Throughout the 1990s and 2000s, there has been a great debate about whether to call the island nation "China" or "Taiwan." The fact that nationalism has become contested in Taiwan reveals a fundamental shift in power, one that has implications for the lives of ordinary Taiwanese people, for the geopolitical struggles in the Pacific, and even for anthropology. As the managers of ideology in Taiwan struggle for power, the meaning of Taiwan's place in the world is debated. Since the Taiwan Strait continues to be one of the world's geopolitical hot spots, a bottom-up study of Taiwan's national question is crucial.

Nation building has obviously been the core of the struggle in Taiwan. This study thus looks at the nation as a human construction, much in the sense meant by Benedict Anderson in *Imagined Communities* (1991). Calling nations "imagined" does not mean that they are imaginary or illusory. It means rather that nations are subjectively imagined or constructed, as the people who constitute them grow to feel a sense of connectedness or community with others. Nations are thus constructed through print journalism, maps, censuses, and museums and other institutions that demarcate the boundaries of national communities. States need to create a sense of identity, what Michel-Rolph Trouillot (2003: 90) calls an "identification effect," to gain legitimacy and popular consent from their citizens. National identity, however, is often contested and negotiated by different groups of people with interests that may diverge from those of the state.

In many national contexts, the state and the ruling classes have thus met resistance as they try to turn their national aspirations into nationalist identities. It has been just as difficult, for example, to construct a French identity in Corsica or a Canadian identity in Québec as it has been to create a Chinese identity in Taiwan. As in situations of class dominance, there are two ways in which the state and ruling classes can maintain power in these situations. The first is through domination and brute force, as confirmed by Mr. Chhoa in his account of Taiwan's February 28 Massacre. The second is through the social process that Italian Communist Antonio Gramsci called hegemony. Hegemony is

> the "spontaneous" consent given by the great masses of the population to the general direction imposed on social life by the dominant fundamental group; this consent is "historically" caused by the prestige (and subsequent confidence) which the dominant group enjoys because of its position and function in the world of production. (Gramsci 1971: 12)

Hegemony is exercised through ideology, "a conception of the world that is implicitly manifest in art, in law, in economic activity and in all manifestations of individual and collective life" (Gramsci 1971: 328). Ideologies based on culture often convince the populace that certain behaviors and loyalties to specific institutions are either more natural or more prestigious than other options that might arise, as Eric Wolf demonstrated in contexts ranging from Aztec Mexico to Nazi Germany (Wolf 1999). Eric Hobsbawm and his colleagues have similarly shown how nations are constructed through the invention of tradition (Hobsbawm and Ranger 1983). They demonstrate that even apparently ancient traditions, such as royal processions in England and kilts in Scotland, are relatively recent innovations promoted in a context of identity building and national construction. In this book, I make the case that "Chinese family firms" are similarly an invention of tradition in Taiwan. This does not mean that small firms did not dominate the Taiwanese economy in the 1970s, as they clearly did and still do. The labeling of them as Chinese, however, was an attempt to incorporate them into the national imagination of the ruling Chinese Nationalist Party.

Yet hegemonies are never complete, and cultural ideologies can be contested, just as Mr. Chhoa did when I approached him with my questions about Chinese culture in his life. From an anthropological perspective, Nicolas Dirks, Geoff Eley, and Sherry Ortner argue strongly that it is impossible "to establish a neutral ground for culture that would itself be exempt from the struggles, claims, contests and chaos of the political world" (Dirks, Eley, and Ortner 1994: 25). Many of the tanners of Taiwan would surely agree. The goal of the anthropologist, therefore, is to render visible the struggles and contests of power that lie beyond power and are so often masked by it.

Culture is highly contested precisely because it implicates individual and collective rights and obligations, particularly in terms of national and class interests. In certain historical circumstances, as we have seen in Taiwan during the past three decades, lower or subaltern groups can develop an awareness of unequal power relations and begin to develop a cultural framework of their own. As Gramsci said, "The lower classes, historically on the defensive, can only achieve self-awareness via a series of negation, via their consciousness of the identity and class limits of their enemy" (Gramsci 1971: 273). It is their mission to develop new forms of culture and to challenge the power relations that oppress them. Both of these dynamics can be observed in workplaces and other social contexts in Taiwan, where identity has become so central to social and political life.

AN ETHNOGRAPHY OF IDENTITY

Of course, individuals embrace more than national, ethnic, and cultural identities. Individuals also have gender, sexual, class, regional, religious, and political identities that simultaneously mark them as members of one group and exclude them from others. In each of these cases, identity is rooted not in primordial communities or nations but in "a mobile, often unstable relation of difference" (Gupta and Ferguson 1997: 13). As writers from Marx to Foucault have demonstrated, identities are confirmed, maintained, and deepened through collective experiences of domination and resistance. Yet in a globalized world, identities now transform national boundaries in unexpected ways (Appadurai 1996).

From family compounds and sites of production to nation-states, identities become inscribed on space through both collective struggle and individual daily practice. This can be seen not only in national monuments (Lefebvre 1991 [1974]: 222) and cities (Pred 1990) but also through such seemingly mundane structures as small factories and irrigation systems. What matters most are the ways in which identity is inscribed on places, and how those identities are contested at local and national levels. Since identities and nationalisms are produced and understood through narratives (Bhabha 1990), life histories, interviews, and simply spending time with people are excellent ways to understand how such identities evolve and then contribute to social change. The goal of this book is thus to explore how ordinary Taiwanese people—rural tanners and their families—create, reproduce, and enact identities in their everyday lives.

OUTLINE OF THE BOOK

John and Jean Comaroff remind us that "no ethnography can ever hope to penetrate beyond the surface planes of everyday life, to plumb its invisible forms, unless it is informed by the historical imagination" (Comaroff and Comaroff 1992: xi). This book thus opens with a discussion of Taiwanese history, especially the national and political context that led to the development of Taiwan as an "island of bosses" (Shieh 1992). I have intentionally woven together stories told by tanners and verified the "facts" against archival files of the leather tanning industry and historical accounts. When tanners retell this history, they emphasize that Taiwan has not always been part of China; it has been colonized by the Dutch, the Manchurian Ch'ing Dynasty, the Japanese, and finally the Chinese Nationalist Party. The historical subject of the Taiwanese emerges from these narratives, inscribing a new national and culture identity on the storytellers.

In Chapter 3, I discuss social life in southern Taiwan, touching on ethnic relations, education, religion, and family life. I show how the Chinese Nationalist Party has reached into the most intimate arenas of Taiwanese life, including the workplace, and justified its rule with a hegemonic discourse of Chinese culture. I also explain how democratization has permitted resistance, including the quest for other forms of identity.

The remaining chapters examine the leather tanning industry from the perspectives of its different actors. Chapters 4 and 5, on family firms and corporations, look at the diversity of firms in the industry, challenging cultural arguments that link firm organization to familial Chinese culture. These chapters take primarily the perspectives of the bosses, how they position themselves in relation to cultural and national narratives about the family firm as a marker of national identity. Chapter 6 takes a gender perspective, surveying the same industry from the perspective of wives, daughters, and daughters-in-law.

The remaining chapters look beyond the family. Chapter 7 explores workers' perspectives and how Chinese culture influences Taiwan's labor movement. Ironically, this is an arena in which the Confucian ideal of harmonious relations is cited as a justification for the absence of labor unions. However, a closer look at the industry reveals that consensus on labor issues is attained through other means. Chapter 8 examines what happens to identities and cultural discourses as Taiwanese tanners move across the Taiwan Strait into China or even farther abroad. Finally, the concluding chapter explains how the people of southern Taiwan used the electoral system after the end of martial law to create a new space for their imagined nation of Taiwan.

Notes

1. I continued to live in Taiwan from August 1998 to August 2001, during which time I conducted a postdoctoral research project on women entrepreneurs at the Institute of Sociology at Academia Sinica. I made additional field visits for four months in 2002 and went to Taiwan as a member of a Canadian parliamentary election observer team in March 2004. This book is a product of all of those observations, albeit with a strong emphasis on the first fieldwork experience.

2. The names of all research participants and their businesses are pseudonyms, and identifying details in their narratives have been changed to ensure anonymity.

3. See Kondo (1990) and Rofel (1999) for similar ethnographies on how identities are crafted in Japanese and Chinese workplaces.

CHAPTER TWO

HISTORICAL CONTEXTS

The nations of Southeast Asia, including Taiwan, have been shaped by centuries of colonialism, transformations in property and market relations, industrialization, and incorporation into a global economy. These political economic forces have required individuals, communities, ethnic groups, and nations to constantly redefine their identities and defend their own interests in rapidly changing circumstances. The changing boundaries of identity are visible in the work histories of Taiwanese entrepreneurs as they link their own personal quests to larger national narratives.

This chapter has two main purposes. First, it provides a brief introduction to Taiwan's geography, climate, population, and history for readers unfamiliar with the region. The historical section presents the processes by which Taiwan was incorporated into global trade networks, developed an industrial structure of flexible "family" firms, and constructed a national identity in a context of imperial conquest and violence. Since it is by necessity incomplete, interested readers are referred to other historical studies.[1] Since this book focuses on leather tanning, more details are provided on the history of that industry, one that clearly reveals the shifts in Taiwan's political economy over a long period of time. This industry is of particular interest to Taiwan studies because leather is arguably Taiwan's oldest export product.

The second purpose of this chapter is to demonstrate how historical narratives provide the raw material from which identity is woven. My first lessons in Taiwanese history took place in the leather tanneries of southern Taiwan, as the tanners brought up such important issues as their aboriginal ancestry, foreign occupation, the modernization drives of the Japanese state, the tragedy of the February 28 Massacre and White Terror, land reform, economic change, and eventually democratic reform. The historical background provided here is thus constructed upon the narratives of the tanners. Day after day, these business-men took time from their busy schedules to share with me their lives and pro-vide impromptu lessons on Taiwanese history, with an enthusiasm that would be unusual in North America. To reflect this ethnographic context, I have con-structed this chapter around their national narratives. Their retelling of these narratives, which happens in many social contexts, is part of their project of identity construction and should be understood as such.

GEOGRAPHY, CLIMATE, AND POPULATION

Taiwan is a sweet potato–shaped island of 36,000 square kilometers in South-east Asia. It is situated between China to the west, Japan to the north, and the Philippines to the south. Part of the mountainous island chain formed at the collision of the Eurasian and the Philippine tectonic plates, it is the largest body of land between Japan and the Philippines. The most important feature of Taiwan's topography is the central range of steep mountains running from the northeast corner to the southern tip of the island. The plains, where most communities, farms, and industries are located, constitute only about 31 per-cent of the island's surface area. Due to its lush vegetation and stunning land-scape, Portuguese explorers in the seventeenth century called it *Ihla Formosa,* or "beautiful island." This name is still claimed with pride by many Taiwanese.

Taiwan's climate is semitropical in the north and tropical in the south. The field research for this book was conducted in communities in the Chianan and Pingtung Plains of southern Taiwan. The Chianan Plain, extending from Changhua to Kaohsiung, makes up 12 percent of the total land area of Tai-wan and is the country's agricultural heartland. Climatic differences between the north and south contributed to the development of the tanning industry in the Chianan and Pingtung Plains. The southern city of Kaohsiung, for ex-ample, has an average annual temperature of 24.4 degrees Celsius and an av-erage of 97 rainy days annually. Taipei, on the other hand, has an average temperature of 22 degrees and rains on average 182 days a year (Government Information Office 1997: 8). In the early days of the industry, when hides were dried outdoors in the sun, this climatic difference led the Japanese gov-ernment to locate tanneries in the south.

Taiwan has a population of 22.5 million people. Taiwan's population is usually described in terms of four main ethnic groups. Like all ethnic groups, they are historically constituted and self-ascriptive, their borders being nego-tiated through relations with others (Barth 1969). Since ethnicity permeates Taiwanese society and strongly influences national events (Gates 1981: 241), a study of Taiwan must begin with an understanding of these dynamics.

Austronesian aborigines, whose ancestors have lived in Taiwan for 12,000 to 15,000 years, make up approximately 2 percent of the population.[2] The descendents of Holo-speaking settlers from Fujian Province on the Chinese mainland, who began immigrating to Taiwan in the seventeenth century, now constitute 73 percent of the population. Descendents of the Hakka-speaking immigrants from Guangdong Province make up 12 percent of the population. Together the Holo and Hakka are referred to as "Native Taiwanese" to distinguish them from later arrivals. After the Communists took control of China, another 1 to 2 million Chinese came to Taiwan. These newcomers and their descendents, referred to as Mainlanders, now make up 13 percent of the population.[3] Most of southern Taiwan, with the exception of the districts surrounding military bases in Kaohsiung, is composed of more than 90 percent Holo Taiwanese. All of the participants in this study, unless mentioned otherwise, are Holo Taiwanese. Their ethnic identity has strongly influenced their views on Taiwan, and those views are reflected in this ethnography more than any other.

A HISTORICAL OVERVIEW

The Dutch Era (1624–1661)

Until the seventeenth century, Taiwan was inhabited by Austronesian aborigines who subsisted on deer hunting and swidden agriculture. The island's location on potentially lucrative regional trade routes and its ready supply of deer hides gradually attracted new occupants, including a mix of Japanese, Chinese, and Korean sea-traders who set up small settlements on the southwest coast in what is now Tainan. By the beginning of the seventeenth century, the aborigines were selling 200,000 deer hides a year to these traders, who sold skins, deer meat, and fish products to China and Japan. Taiwan at this time was claimed by neither China nor Japan.

The Europeans were the first to see commercial value in Taiwan. As part of their ambitions in East Asia, the Dutch attempted to take over the Pescadore Islands in 1622 but were repelled by Chinese forces. Seeing little value in Taiwan, however, the Ming government gave the Dutch permission to take the island. The Dutch established their first forts in Taiwan in 1624, in the region that is now Tainan. The Spanish briefly established a settlement in northern Taiwan in 1626 but ceded it to the Dutch in 1642.

At first, the Dutch were primarily interested in deer meat and skins and focused on the hide trade. In the midcentury, they were exporting more than 60,000 hides per year from Taiwan (Wills 1999: 93). Nonetheless, unsustainable hunting eventually decreased the deer population, and the Dutch began developing the area around Tainan into a more comprehensive trade center and agricultural colony. The chief export products at the time were deer hides and sugar, destined primarily for the Japanese market. As the aboriginal population was insufficient for their labor requirements, they brought in Holo-speaking

Table 2.1   Time Line of Major Events in Taiwanese History

Prior to 1624	Taiwan populated by Austronesian peoples; limited Chinese settlement, but no state presence
1590	Portuguese sailors name Taiwan *Ihla Formosa* ("beautiful island")
1624–1641	Spanish colonial presence in northern Taiwan
1624–1661	Dutch colonial presence in southern Taiwan, migration from China begins in earnest
1644	Manchurian Ch'ing Dynasty established in China
1661	Ming Loyalist Koxinga retreats to Taiwan
1661–1683	Reign of Koxinga and later his son on Taiwan
1683	Ch'ing Dynasty takes control of Taiwan
1683–1895	Ch'ing rule of Taiwan, further migration from China
1875	Ch'ing administration expanded to Eastern Taiwan
1887	Taiwan made a province of China
1894–1895	Sino-Japanese War
1895	Taiwan ceded to Japan in Treaty of Shimonoseki
1895–1945	Japanese administration and modernization of Taiwan
1911	Revolution in China leads to founding of the Republic of China
1912	Founding of the Chinese Nationalist Party
1945	Conclusion of World War II, the Chinese Nationalist Party under Chiang Kai-shek takes Taiwan
1947	Demands for Taiwanese self-rule are met with violent repression, martial law begins
1949	Communist Revolution in China, Republic of China retreats to Taiwan
1951	Land Reform breaks up landlord class, gives land to tillers
1971	Republic of China loses United Nations seat
1972	Nixon visits China, issues Shanghai Communique recognizing the People's Republic of China
1975	Death of Chiang Kai-shek, Chiang Ching-kuo becomes president
1979	US ends diplomatic relations with Taiwan, Kaohsiung Incident
1986	Foundation of the Democratic Progressive Party
1987	End of Martial Law
1988	Chiang Ching-kuo dies and is succeeded by Lee Teng-hui
1996	Lee Teng-hui elected in first direct presidential election
2000	Chen Shui-bian elected
2004	Chen Shui-bian re-elected

settlers from China's Fujian Province to open up farmland and cultivate sugar. Taiwanese people now remember the Dutch period as their first experience with foreign occupation.

The Reign of the Cheng Family (1661–1683)
Due to political turmoil in China, Dutch rule in Taiwan did not last long. In 1644, the Manchus took over China and established the Ch'ing Dynasty. Although the Ming emperor himself fled to Southeast Asia and was killed in Vietnam in 1661, Ming loyalists continued to resist the Manchus. One of the most powerful rebels acting in the name of the Ming Dynasty was Cheng Cheng-kung, also known by the English name of Koxinga. Koxinga was born in 1624 to a Japanese mother and a Holo-speaking father from Taiwan. Coming from a wealthy trading family with commercial links extending from Nagasaki to Macao, he commanded a significant private naval force. Throughout the 1650s, Koxinga fought the Manchus fiercely, but he was eventually defeated by Manchu troops. He retreated to Taiwan, where his navy defeated the Dutch.

Koxinga brought with him a massive influx of immigrants from China. Before his arrival, the Taiwanese population of 100,000 people included only 20,000–30,000 Holo-speakers, who lived amidst the aborigines on the coastal plains. Koxinga brought in an additional population of 30,000 soldiers. When the Ch'ing Dynasty sealed off the east coast of China, forbidding settlement near the sea, an additional 60,000–70,000 Chinese fled to Taiwan. Most of the plains on the west coast of Taiwan were opened up for agriculture and taken over by Chinese refugees. Koxinga's family did not relinquish their dream of recapturing China, and his son spent most of his career on unsuccessful military expeditions in Fujian. Finally, in 1683, the Ch'ing military took over Taiwan, making it administratively a part of Fujian Province.

Taiwan Under Manchu Rule (1683–1895)
Taiwan, however, proved to be a difficult place to rule. Since Taiwan had long been a haven for pirates and rebels, the Ch'ing government took strict measures in the early decades of their rule to keep the island peaceful. In the early years of Ch'ing rule, immigration to the island was restricted. From 1684 to 1788, Chinese women were not permitted to immigrate to Taiwan (Brown 1996: 51). Ignoring laws limiting contact between Chinese and aborigines, especially the ban on mixed marriages, many Chinese men sought out aboriginal women as mates and wives. Taiwanese people on the Chianan Plain, including many of the tanners, still refer proudly to their mixed ancestry by saying "We have Tang Mountain (China) fathers, not Tang Mountain mothers." Many contemporary Taiwanese customs, such as the chewing of betel nuts, were learned from the aborigines.

In the eighteenth and nineteenth centuries, the Ch'ing court began to encourage further settlement of Taiwan. The majority of immigrants settled down as tenants on land sold or granted by the imperial state in blocks to large landlords. At this time, Taiwan imported manufactured consumer goods from the Chinese mainland and exported agricultural products, primarily sugar, tea, rice, and camphor, a product used in Chinese medicine. By the late nineteenth century, the Taiwanese deer population had been largely exterminated by hunting, and the deer hide trade declined accordingly.

Due to Taiwan's strategic location, foreign powers began to covet the island. In the 1870s, Japan began to sign treaties with aborigines and established a military presence in eastern Taiwan, an area not administered by China until 1875. The French briefly occupied northern Taiwan during the Sino-French War of 1884–1885, but upon victory France relinquished it to China in return for control of Annan in Indochina. Faced with these challenges, China had no choice but to modernize Taiwan and fortify their administrative presence on the island. In 1887, Taiwan was made a province of China, with Liu Ming-chuan as the first governor.[4] Governor Liu implemented a "self-strengthening movement," encouraging technological development and the introduction of modern institutions.

During this time, Taipei became Taiwan's commercial and administrative center. Ports were improved, the first stretches of railroad were laid, the first telegraph lines were put into place, and some modern schools were established. These early modernization attempts, however, proved insufficient to keep the island in Chinese hands, especially in the face of Japanese imperialist ambitions. Interestingly, none of the tanners ever discussed this period with me; they focused instead on the modernization that occurred under Japanese influence. This silence, of course, is as much a part of their national identity as the narratives on the benefits of Japanese modernization.[5]

Taiwan as a Japanese Colony (1895–1945)

In 1894–1895, Japan and China fought over Korea in the Sino-Japanese War. In a humiliating defeat for the Ch'ing Dynasty, Japan swept through Korea, invaded China, and made it as far as Shandong Province. In the ensuing Treaty of Shimonoseki, China made numerous concessions, including the cession of Taiwan and the Pescadore Islands to Japan "in perpetuity." The people of Taiwan did not yield easily to Japan. After the signing of the Treaty of Shimonoseki, Taiwanese leaders briefly declared Taiwan to be an independent Republic of Formosa and tried in vain to get foreign support.

The Japanese troops who arrived in June 1895 had to face local resistance and guerrilla warfare. Only in November did the Japanese finally secure the entire island, but sporadic resistance continued until 1902. In the first few years of Japanese rule, the Japanese relied on the strong hand of the military police to enforce peace and order. In 1905, they took the first population census and set up a household registration system to better control the population.

In their fifty years of rule, the Japanese laid down railroad tracks along the west coast, completed a road transportation network, and modernized the island's major ports. They set up an efficient irrigation system and built hydroelectric plants. They built hospitals and improved the sanitary conditions of the island. They established libraries, schools, and technical institutes, raising the educational level of the local people. By 1944, approximately 70 percent of all school-age children were enrolled in school, clear evidence of the success of Japanese educational reform (Tsurumi 1977). Most of the population was taught Japanese, and the brightest students were often sent to Japan for higher education. To this day, older Taiwanese people refer proudly to their Japanese education and to their identification with Japan as signs of their modernity and cultural superiority relative to those who came later from China.

Japanese institutional reform laid the foundation for Taiwanese capitalism (Gold 1986). Much-needed economic and legal reforms encouraged commerce and investment. Measurements were unified, a stable currency was introduced, and the Bank of Taiwan was established to encourage savings and provide capital for agriculture and industry. After centuries of crime and violence, law and order were established through an efficient police force and judicial system. In 1898, the Japanese conducted the first land survey. They abolished the old land tenure system, introducing a modern system of property rights that included the right to buy and sell land. State industries were established to ensure revenue for Japan. The sugar industry became the most important state industry (see Ka 1995), but the colonial state also established monopolies in such commodities as salt, camphor, tobacco, alcohol, and leather.

During the Japanese period, a distinction was made between the ruling Japanese and the local Taiwanese. All major industries, including sugar refining, paper, cement, and even leather tanning were directly or indirectly owned by Japanese conglomerates, albeit sometimes with local partners. In 1941, more than 90 percent of registered corporations with paid-up capital of at least 200,000 yen were owned by Japanese capitalists.[6] From 1912 to 1923, Taiwanese firms without Japanese partners were even prohibited from using the word *kaisha* ("corporation") in their names. As a result, most Taiwanese-owned businesses remained small (Numazaki 1986: 489). These small businesses included some tanning workshops using craft-production techniques. Nonetheless, the Japanese occupation is widely remembered in Taiwan as a time of modernity, public order, and prosperity. Like many Taiwanese, tanners proudly tout the achievements of their families during that time.

The Leather Industry Under Japanese Occupation
The modern-day Taiwanese leather industry was born during the Japanese occupation, as both local Taiwanese and Japanese entrepreneurs invested, often jointly, in new enterprises. The first mechanized tannery in Taiwan was

Figure 2.1   Japanese-era building. Many examples of Japanese-style architecture in Taiwan attest to the city's Japanese legacy.

established in 1912 by Lin Ching-hsiu, who founded the Taiwan Leather Processing Joint Venture Tannery in Taipei with Oarai Tsutomu, a Japanese partner. In 1919, Japanese capitalists in Tainan established the Taiwan Leather Joint Stock Company. In 1932, Tsutomu bought out the Taiwan Leather Processing Joint Venture Tannery. In the same year, it was reorganized into a stock-issuing corporation, a legal option unavailable to Taiwanese-owned firms, since colonial law stipulated that stock-issuing corporations had to be controlled by Japanese capital.

By 1938, two Japanese-owned stock-issuing corporations dominated the industry. They each employed more than twenty workers, whereas the largest Taiwanese-owned tannery employed only ten craftsmen. Japanese firms ran their tanneries as modern factories with hired labor, whereas the smaller Taiwanese-owned firms were usually family businesses that relied on an apprentice system for craft-based (that is, nonmechanical) production.

In 1938, the entire industry was restructured. In order to facilitate the supply of leather to the military, the Japanese state began to purchase Taiwanese-owned tanneries, putting them under the monopoly control of the state-run Taiwan Animal Products Development Company. The Japanese government also built large new tanneries in Taipei and Kaohsiung. In order to boost production, the Animal Products Development Company established a leather research institute. The state put strict controls on pigskin supplies, requiring slaughterhouses to supply pigskins to the state agricultural bureau rather than selling them with the pork to the general public. The state also requisitioned tanning agents, requiring lumberyards to collect and deliver the bark of osmosia and horsetail trees (Li 1971).

The Tiu Family: Building Up from Japanese Roots

Many wealthy Taiwanese families acquired their personal fortunes during the Japanese period. Twenty-eight out of southern Taiwan's seventy-two leather tanneries (39 percent) either have direct roots in the Japanese period or were started by tanners with experience gained in Japanese-run tanneries. Some of them still send family members and management to Japan for further training in the industry, reinforcing a strong sense of identity with the former colonial power.

These families, with capital and expertise gained from cooperation with the Japanese, have been an innovative force in the industry. One example is the powerful Tiu family of Tainan. Tiu Oan-pin, the family patriarch, started his business career by running a hotel in Tainan. In cooperation with a Japanese partner, he invested in a lumberyard and began to amass a small fortune. Upon his death, the capital gained from the timber venture supported his three sons in their respective business ventures.

The second son took over the lumberyard directly. The third son went into the pharmaceutical business and now runs a large factory that produces Western medicine. The elder son, Tiu Kim-hoat, took a degree from a technical school during the Japanese period and became interested in leather tanning. At the time, the Japanese operated a leather tannery in Tainan County, using vegetable tanning techniques on pigskins with chestnut tannin imported from Japan. In 1945, when the Japanese left, Tiu Kim-hoat bought out the tannery, now known as Formosa Leather.

Tiu Kim-hoat had four sons and four daughters. The four daughters married out of the family, one of them to a hide trader. The elder son is now the president of Formosa Leather, and the fourth son works in management at the company. The second son left the company and established a company producing baseball gloves. Formosa Leather, with a registered capital of $67.5 million (New Taiwan, or NT) and 218 workers, is now one of the largest companies in the industry. Formosa Leather's innovative research and development department has gained a reputation as the island's "Leather Research Institute."

Most of Taiwan's leading tanneries were started by managers and technicians who first gained experience at Formosa Leather but then left to start their own companies. The experience of Japanese colonialism, which included the introduction of modern Japanese management, thus had a lasting influence on the Taiwanese leather tanning industry as well as on the identities of its leading entrepreneurs. By the 1920s, a nascent Taiwanese identity, or the idea of Taiwan as a nation distinct from both China and Japan, was already forming (Chang 2003: 25).

Transition to Chinese Nationalist Party Rule

At the conclusion of World War II, the victorious Allied forces ceded Taiwan to their Chinese ally, General Chiang Kai-shek, who declared it to be a province of the Republic of China under the rule of the Chinese Nationalist Party.[7] When Chinese troops arrived on the island at the end of 1945, they were warmly welcomed by the local people who initially viewed them as liberators from foreign domination. These hopes, however, quickly dissipated as the local people, accustomed to well-disciplined Japanese soldiers, suddenly faced poorly dressed, uneducated Chinese troops, many of whom had never seen the modern conveniences that the Taiwanese took for granted. Several tanners recounted to me a common joke:

> There was once a Mainlander who saw a Taiwanese using tap water. He went to the hardware store and bought a tap. The next day he returned it, angrily saying that the vendor had sold him broken merchandise. The store owner asked what was wrong. The Mainlander said, "My neighbor's tap in the wall produces water, but when I screwed this one into the wall no water came out."

As they had done in China, Chinese soldiers sometimes terrorized local populations by stealing, raping, and looting. The new government was not much better. The new governor, Chen Yi, seized all Japanese property, selling off large stocks of equipment and goods for personal profit. Relations between the incoming Chinese forces and the local population were further strained by language differences. The Chinese newcomers spoke Mandarin Chinese and various other dialects, whereas the local people spoke only Taiwanese languages and Japanese. Disillusioned by violent troops and corrupt officials, and unable to communicate effectively with the newcomers in any language, the local people began to perceive the Chinese Nationalist Party as yet another occupying force and the Mainlanders as a distinct ethnic group.

The Taiwanese started to refer to the changeover as a case of "the dogs leaving and the pigs coming." One person told me, "Neither are human, but at least dogs will bark and help you guard your house. Pigs don't do anything but sleep and eat." With growing misunderstanding, it was just a matter of time before conflict broke out.

On February 28, 1947, a woman peddler was injured in a scuffle that broke out when Taipei City Monopoly Board officers and policemen tried to confiscate the contraband cigarettes she was selling on the street, as well as the money she had earned. When neighbors rushed to her defense, one of the investigators shot into the crowd and fatally injured a bystander. As news of the event spread, violent conflicts occurred between Chinese forces and the local population all over the island. In the weeks that followed, the Taiwanese launched an opposition movement to protest oppressive aspects of Chinese

Figure 2.2   Taiwanese people remember the victims of the February 28 massacre in annual ceremonies, such as this one in Taipei.

Nationalist Party rule. They set up "February 28 Resolution Committees," demanding an investigation of the incident, democratic and economic reforms, and limited self-rule.

Chinese Nationalist Party governor Chen Yi pretended to negotiate with the Resolution Committees, yet actually requested military reinforcement from Chiang Kai-shek in China. On March 8, troops arrived on Taiwan and responded with force, first killing indiscriminately on the streets and then rounding up opposition leaders for execution. Casualty numbers are still unknown but have been estimated at over 20,000. Those arrested later were subject to torture and imprisonment. Martial law, established in 1947, would last until 1987—the longest period of martial law in human history.[8]

The influence of the February 28 Massacre on Taiwanese national identity cannot be overemphasized, as the event firmly seeded the idea of opposing Chinese and Taiwanese identities in the minds of an entire generation (Chang 2003: 46–47; Edmondson 2002). Having experienced the Chinese as violent conquerors, many Taiwanese identified with the father of former presidential candidate Peng Ming-min, who denounced his Chinese identity and hoped that his descendents would marry foreigners to remove Chinese "blood" from the lineage (Chang 2003: 46). Taiwanese tanners, like other members of their community, still assert a non-Chinese identity through constant memory of the February 28 Massacre, and some of them recall witnessing acts of violence themselves. They use the narrative to contrast the efficiency and social order of the Japanese with the violence of the Chinese. The mere retelling of the narrative reinforces their identity as non-Chinese.

American Influence and the "Economic Miracle"

On October 1, 1949, the Communists took over China. Like Koxinga some three hundred years earlier, Chiang Kai-shek's Chinese Nationalist Party was forced to retreat to the island of Taiwan. At first, it appeared that the United States under President Truman would disengage from the region, allowing Chiang Kai-shek to protect his own interests against Communist China (Spence 1990: 527). In 1950, however, with the outbreak of the Korean War, the United States decided to protect Chiang Kai-shek and his forces as part of an Asian front against communism. The intervention of U.S. forces in the Taiwan Strait prevented the Communists from taking over Taiwan and helped solidify Chinese Nationalist rule of Taiwan in spite of the fact that they were no longer welcomed by many of the local population.

Economically, the Chinese Nationalist Party found itself on the relatively solid foundation laid by the Japanese. The island already possessed a good transportation network, financial and commercial institutions, an educated populace accustomed to industrialization, and basic industries. The Nationalist state received a massive influx of U.S. aid. In the 1950s, U.S. economic aid alone equaled about 6 percent of Taiwan's GNP and nearly 40 percent of gross investment (Wade 1990: 82). American military protection, aid, and technical advice further promoted economic and industrial growth in Taiwan (Barrett 1988). American-style modernity became a new dimension of identity in Taiwan, although not without resistance (Chang 2003: 47–48).

Just as they had been excluded from political power in the Japanese era, the Native Taiwanese, over 80 percent of the island's population, found themselves excluded again under Chinese Nationalist rule. Under the pretext that the Taiwanese people did not speak adequate Mandarin Chinese, the Mainlanders virtually monopolized political power and key industries, leaving the Native Taiwanese to focus on small industry and entrepreneurship (Gates 1981). Native Taiwanese were naturally resentful of their lack of power as well as the new language policies that forced them once again to learn the language of an incoming power (see Chapter 3). Although this ethnic-based repression contributed further to Taiwanese identity (Chang 2003: 48), there was little room for protest under martial law. The Native Taiwanese focused their energies on entrepreneurial efforts as one of the few avenues left open to them.

Tanning Hides Under Nationalist Rule: The Early Years

The transition to Chinese rule brought great changes in the leather industry. Monopoly policies established by the Japanese were abolished, and the leather research institute was closed. Freed from the legal constraints of the Japanese state, which during the war had barred Taiwanese entrepreneurs from entering the industry, local people began establishing new leather tanneries. Many were entrepreneurs who had cooperated with the Japanese or workers with experience in Japanese-run tanneries.

Some leather tanneries were moved to Taiwan from the mainland and were established primarily in the northern region of the island. One such tannery was Hsin Yuanchang Tannery in Taoyuan, originally Yuanchang Tannery of Shanghai, whose owner brought technology and an entire staff of well-qualified technicians with him when he fled from the Communists in 1949. Mainland tanners in that period made Taoyuan famous for leather production (Taiwan Region Leather Tanning Association 1989: 3). The south of the island, however, remained dominated by Taiwanese-owned firms. In my visits to sixty-eight southern tanneries, I encountered no Hakka or aboriginal tanners and only one mainland tanner. Interestingly, he made the strong argument that he had not come to Taiwan with Chiang Kai-shek, thus distancing himself from the political connotations of Mainlander identity.

Growth of the leather tanning and other industries was encouraged by land reform. After stipulating rent reductions and distributing public lands to farmers, the Nationalist state began an ambitious land-to-the-tiller reform in 1951, partly in order to eliminate the powerful landlord class that had benefited from collaboration with the Japanese. The amount of agricultural land that could be held by any family was fixed by law, and surplus land was redistributed to the tillers. Former landlords were compensated with ration coupons for agricultural inputs and stock in state-run industries, which they initially perceived as worthless. The land reform thus reduced the economic burden on small farmers, redirected capital resources to industry, and eliminated the landlord class. These reforms met with little resistance from the landlords, who were still cowed by memories of the violence of 1947.

Land reform encouraged the growth of small industry in Taiwan by reducing the rent burdens faced by small farmers and giving land to rural families. No longer required to pay high rents, many farmers used their new land and higher net incomes to invest in small manufacturing undertakings. The redistribution of land, which gave rural families direct ownership of the land they worked, is thus the main reason that rural Taiwan became dotted with small factories and workshops.

The main obstacle to growth in the industry was the import substitution policy of the early 1950s. Designed to protect nascent local industries from the competition of foreign manufacturers, import substitution policies placed high tariffs on imported goods. Most companies were not permitted to exchange money or purchase foreign inputs. Such policies had a harmful impact on the local leather industry, since the island has only a small livestock population and could not provide a sufficient supply of raw hides. About two-thirds of the small tanneries that opened up after 1945 were eventually forced to stop production within a few years because of the difficulties in securing raw materials.

Figure 2.3   Rawhides, Kaohsiung.

Leather industry leaders, however, organized themselves and lobbied for change. In 1948, Ke Fu-chiang, recently arrived from China, organized the Taiwan Region Leather Tanning Association.[9] Ta Chung-hwa Tannery, founded just after the Chinese takeover, was selected in 1951 for a subsidy from the newly established Industrial Council to purchase tanning equipment from Germany. Ta Chung-hwa and another large northern tannery lobbied the Industrial Council to restrict the importation of finished leather but permit the importation of raw hides. Their main argument was that leather is a military necessity, and the development of a domestic industry would allow the military to conserve scarce foreign currency. In 1953, the government finally permitted leather tanneries to use foreign currency to import raw hides, a step that allowed the tanning industry to expand. By 1958, Taiwan had more than one hundred leather tanneries (Taiwan Region Leather Tanning Association 1989: 4–5).

In the 1960s, the emphasis of industrial policy changed to export promotion policies designed to support industrial expansion, boost foreign currency reserves, and attract foreign investment in export-oriented sectors. Newly constructed industrial parks provided industrial land at low prices to entrepreneurs, and export-processing zones were created to attract foreign investment. Tariff rebates and export tax incentives encouraged companies to seek international markets. In 1970, the China External Trade Development Council (CETRA) was formed to promote the island's products through a trade center in Taipei and in overseas offices. These policies fueled unprecedented economic growth. Economic growth was accompanied by low inflation, low unemployment, and relatively low income disparities, giving rise to what has been called the "Taiwanese miracle."[10]

Leather tanneries benefited from export promotion policies. In 1979, the government identified leather tanning as one of Taiwan's fifty key industries, a designation that allowed tanneries to secure low-interest bank loans. With state subsidies, the Leather Tanning Association supported sending tanners to study tanning in Germany and Japan. They also sponsored foreign leather experts to come to Taiwan and lecture on technological innovations (Taiwan Region Leather Tanning Association 1989: 63–64).

For most tanneries, however, the tariff rebate system had the largest impact. First, finished leather imports were taxed much higher than hide imports, a policy that allowed domestic tanners to produce leather with virtually no competition from imported goods. Finished leather was subject to an import tariff of 50 percent, whereas raw hides were taxed at 18 percent. Furthermore, manufacturers could gain a tariff rebate upon exporting the finished goods (Liang 1986: 87). One tanner told me that tanneries profited from tariff rebates, using creative accounting and forged receipts to maximize their rebates. The difference between what they actually paid in import tariffs and the higher amount that they claimed accounted for a good part of their operating profits.

Export promotion in the shoe industry also encouraged leather tanners by providing an expanding domestic market. In the 1970s, the shoe industry flourished in Taiwan because low wages permitted shoe companies to produce cheaply in that labor-intensive industry. In 1976, Taiwan surpassed Italy to become the world's largest shoe producer. The shoe industry's share of Taiwan's exports rose from 1.8 percent in 1968 to 7.45 percent in 1986 (Skoggard 1996: 56).

The boom in shoe production provided plenty of opportunities for both large and small leather producers. In order to reduce the risk related to fluctuating demand, most tanneries worked through a subcontracting system. When orders rose, they subcontracted out parts of the production process to smaller workshops. The larger tanneries dealt with the shoe factories and distributed subcontracts out to smaller, often family-based workshops. It was relatively easy at the time for workers to save capital, buy a machine or two, and set up a small independent workshop. The prevalence of subcontracting in a variety of industries, including leather tanning, made Taiwan into an island of small bosses (Shieh 1992).[11] The boom, however, did not last long.

Economic Restructuring in the 1980s and 1990s

Economic and political restructuring in the 1980s brought a series of new problems to manufacturers in Taiwan. By the late 1980s, successful export promotion policies had created a massive trade surplus. Under pressure from

Figure 2.4   Leather tanneries. Due to insufficient water treatment, the waters ran blue in this tannery district near Kaohsiung. These tanneries have subsequently been closed down.

the United States, the Nationalist state abandoned many of its protectionist policies and shifted to a free market regime. In 1985, import tariffs were lowered to a rate of 1.25 percent for raw hides, 2 percent for wet-blue hides, and 4 percent for processed leather. Simultaneously, the tariff rebate system was abolished (Liang 1986: 87).

This change in tax incentives had an almost immediate effect on the leather industry. No longer able to benefit from tariff rebates, many producers of less profitable sole leather and pig upper skin leather could no longer make a profit and started producing other products. The production of sole leather dropped so far, in fact, that the Ministry of Economic Affairs stopped publishing production figures for the commodity after 1992. Production of cowhide upper leather and suede, however, were little affected by the change in tax policy (Li 1996: 626).

Production during the export promotion phase rose far more rapidly than the supply of labor, leading to an acute labor shortage. Leather tanneries, with their dangerous and unpleasant work environments, were especially hard hit. Tanners often complained to me about the problems they encounter in finding workers. Primarily due to the unpleasant odors of the tanning process, most new workers usually spend only a few days in the tannery before quitting.

The labor shortage contributed to rising labor costs in Taiwan. The rise in labor costs was further exacerbated by fluctuations in the exchange value of the NT dollar. The high trade surplus itself exerted tremendous pressure on the New Taiwanese dollar, causing the currency to appreciate sharply against the U.S. dollar. The result was a dramatic increase in labor costs measured in U.S. dollars, which weakened Taiwan's competitiveness in labor-intensive export industries such as shoe manufacturing. Average monthly wages more than doubled from 1982 to 1994.

Taiwan's manufacturers have been quick to adapt to these problems. In nearly every industry, there has been a clear trend away from labor-intensive production and toward capital-intensive, high value-added production as manufacturers move labor-intensive production offshore to areas of lower-cost labor, accelerate automation, and promote the production of high value-added products. Labor-intensive consumer goods, once Taiwan's most important export products, declined from 35.6 percent of exports in 1986 to only 18.1 percent in 1993 (Schive 1995: 16). Shoe companies were among the first to leave. By 1989, nearly every shoe factory had cut production and was in the process of moving production to China or Southeast Asia (Skoggard 1996: 64).

This change brought about rapid restructuring in the leather industry. Most tanneries have used automation to make a transition from labor-intensive to capital-intensive production. Beginning in 1989, most large tanneries could also solve the labor shortage problem by hiring foreign workers from Thailand or the Philippines. This solution is expensive, however, as tanneries must provide foreign workers with housing, food, and insurance, in addition to wages. Furthermore, only the medium-size to large factories that meet minimum-size requirements in invested capital and number of workers can legally hire foreign workers. Small factories, even if they also have difficulty in finding workers, are not permitted to hire foreign labor. Large firms are thus in a better position to find workers and meet production goals.

The result of these changes has been a drop in labor costs. Tanners estimate that wages now account for only about 8–10 percent of their production costs. Low wages, therefore, do not provide a significant attraction for Taiwanese tanneries to move abroad. However, some large tanneries have moved abroad in order to be closer to their customers.

With leather and leather product companies leaving Taiwan and the remaining large firms shifting to in-house production with increased automation and teams of foreign workers, the number of subcontracts available to small firms has diminished. With less business, many of the smaller tanneries, once dependent on subcontracting, have been forced to close. The result is that the bottom tier of the subcontracting system, consisting of small family-based leather workshops, has begun to disappear.

Large tanneries with good international connections have actually benefited from the change and even expanded production. Due to the low quality of Chinese leather, most Taiwanese-owned shoe factories in China continue to use Taiwanese leather in their shoes. Both production and exports of high-quality upper leather have increased, even as shoe factories have moved offshore. In 1994, Taiwan exported 41,336,977 kilograms of processed leather, a 7.5 percent increase over 1993 and a 34.6 percent increase over 1992 leather exports (Huang 1995: 534). The main beneficiaries of this trade are the large firms involved in business networks with the shoe factories. Taiwanese tanners, however, have been influenced by political as well as economic change.

Democratic Struggle and Social Change

Beginning in the 1970s, both Native Taiwanese and Mainlander democracy activists began demanding expanded rights for themselves, democratic reform, and even independence from the Republic of China. Two underground magazines, *Formosa Magazine* and *The Eighties* were started by opposition leaders as mouthpieces for these political objectives. To mark the occasion of International Human Rights Day, the editors of *Formosa Magazine* organized a rally in the southern city of Kaohsiung on December 10, 1979. In their speeches, rally organizers gave speeches in the Taiwanese language, an action still perceived as seditious at the time. In an effort to unite all ethnic groups in the democracy movement, feminist lawyer Annette Lu made this appeal:

> It doesn't matter whether you speak Chekiangese or Cantonese, or for that matter Uigur—in as much as we are all in the same boat, we should learn to love each other. Our bonds should be of the heart. Should we not take each other's hand and struggle together for the future of Taiwan? (International Committee for Human Rights in Taiwan 1981: 45)

As crowds shouted out slogans such as "Long live the Taiwanese!" and sang a Taiwanese translation of "We Shall Overcome," they were surrounded and attacked with tear gas by military and riot police. In the days that followed, the office of *Formosa Magazine* was destroyed, and the leaders of the opposition movement were arrested. As control of the press was tightened, the media reported that protesters had started a riot, leaving 183 police injured but reported no civilian casualties.

From March to May 1980, a series of three trials were held in military and civil tribunals to convict opposition leaders and their supporters, even though evidence of torture to extract false confessions was presented. The trials were open to the public and broadcast throughout the media, ironically bringing issues of Taiwanese independence and self-determination into public discourse for the first time. The eight rally leaders, including those who had made speeches in Kaohsiung, were given sentences ranging from a few years to life imprisonment. Among those leaders was Annette Lu, who was represented by lawyer Chen Shui-bian. This fateful rally that brought the opposition into media prominence was later referred to as the Formosa Incident.[12] It galvanized an entire generation of social activists and put the question of national identity at the center of public discourse.

Throughout the 1980s, a nonparty *(dangwai)* movement continued to gain momentum in Taiwan, with the wives of arrested opposition leaders often successfully running for local office. In 1986, the opposition formed the Democratic Progressive Party (DPP), even though opposition parties were still illegal at the time. In 1987, under strong pressure from the *dangwai* movement, Chiang Ching-kuo lifted martial law. In 1991, his handpicked successor, President Lee Teng-hui, suspended the "temporary provisions," a set of measures that, among other things, had forbidden the promotion of Taiwanese independence. Tanners, however, were not necessarily content with the demands of a newly empowered civil society, especially when they conflicted with business imperatives.

Democracy and Its Challenges

Since the end of martial law on July 15, 1987, grassroots pressure groups across Taiwan, once illegal, have advocated a wide range of causes including environmentalism and labor rights (see Chapter 7). In 1997, for example, citizens in Tainan County's Matou Township protested against the water pollution emitted by factories in their local industrial park, including two large leather tanneries. The government has accordingly increased enforcement of pollution guidelines, and some tanneries have been shut down for noncompliance. Several of the tanneries on my initial list had already been shut down before I even began my study. And in August 1997, after I had finished my tannery survey, Kaohsiung County closed four of the tanneries because they had not taken the required measures to reduce water pollution.

Tanners say that government inspectors arrive at tanneries without warning to inspect water treatment facilities. One tanner estimated that he spent about NT$400,000 a month to treat water, but the government is never satisfied and keeps pushing the standards higher. He claimed that environmental standards in Taiwan are "even higher than in the United States," repeating the statement several times for emphasis. Increased enforcement of environmental guidelines has mostly hurt small tanneries. The larger, capital-rich companies can more

Figure 2.5   Environmental protest. Environmentalists protest the planned construction of a nuclear-power plant. The large banner reads, "Taiwan, Our Mother."

easily afford to pay fines or invest in water treatment facilities. Cash-strapped small tanneries, on the other hand, have little choice but to close down production and move on to other endeavors.

In light of these circumstances, small subcontractors are pessimistic about their future. One cool February afternoon, I took the train to Tahu Township, just across the border from Tainan in Kaohsiung County. I found the tannery I was looking for in a small lane off the main highway and walked into the factory compound. There were a few cow skins stretched out on racks to dry, but not a soul was in sight. An old man came out of the house and got on a motorcycle. I walked up to him, smiled, and said hello. Without saying a word, he rode away. I looked in the house. The door was unlocked, but no one was there. I walked alone into the factory. There were two tanning drums, a drying press, and a splitter, and all were silent. As the floor was dry and dusty, I could see that the tanning drums had not been used in a long time. I walked back out to the courtyard, just in time to see the old man coming back. He was chewing a betel nut, and his wrinkled face revealed red stains around his mouth.

I asked him whether it was his factory. He said yes, but he didn't have any business. I pulled out my name card and offered it to him, explaining that I was doing research on the leather industry and would like to interview him. In anger, he spit the last bit of his betel nut into my outstretched hand.

"I have nothing to say because I don't have any business."

"What a shame," I said, trying to express sympathy. "There are not even workers here."

"With no business how can I hire workers?" With that final statement, he turned and walked away, going into the garden to tend his flowers. I wiped the betel juice off my hand, went into the factory, snapped some photos of the idle machines, and continued down the road in search of other tanneries, reflecting on the myriad difficulties of a society in flux.

Notes

1. For general histories, see especially Gold (1986), Kho (1996), Morris (2004), and Rubinstein (1999).

2. For further information on these groups, see Brown (2004) and Shepherd (1993).

3. These statistics come from Corcuff (2002a: 163).

4. Although beyond the scope of this book, there are discrepancies about this date in historical records. They are attributable either to translations of the Ch'ing calendar or to the earlier arrival of Liu Ming-chuan to the island (Chen and Reisman 1972: 610).

5. See Trouillet (1995) on the importance of silence and historiography.

6. Note that ¥200,000 was much more money in 1941 than it is today.

7. There is some doubt about the legal validity of this claim (Chen and Reisman 1972), but that is beyond the scope of this book.

8. For more information on the difficult transition to Chinese rule, including the February 28 Massacre and its influence on Taiwanese national identities, see Arrigo (1998), Chang (2003), Edmondson (2002), Kerr (1965), Lai, Myers, and Wou (1991), Lin (1998), Mendel (1970), Philips (1999, 2003), Rubinstein (1999), and Simon (2003).

9. The name implies that Taiwan is merely a region of the Republic of China. Until the 1990s, all organizations had to use "Republic of China" in their names or refer to Taiwan as a "region" to avoid any possibility of thinking of Taiwan as an independent nation.

10. For an overview of the copious literature on the Taiwan miracle, and a full bibliography, see Wade 1990.

11. This also led to a small body of anthropological literature on small and medium enterprises in Taiwan; see, for example, Greenhalgh (1994), Harrell (1985), Hsiung (1996), Niehoff (1987), Skoggard (1996), and Stites (1982, 1985).

12. For further information on the Formosa Incident, see International Committee for Human Rights in Taiwan (1981).

CHAPTER THREE

SOCIAL BACKGROUND

Ju Tiong-chi was preparing for his geography exam in the office of his father's tannery. Looking at the map of northeast China that he was studying so intently, I noticed that it delineated nine provinces. I told him that I distinctly remembered that there were three provinces in northeast China: Heilongjiang, Jilin, and Liaoning. "I know that the Communists changed the borders, but we have to memorize the old nine provinces for the test," he said, handing me his textbook. I glanced through the pages, pointing out to him that Nanjing was listed as the capital of the Republic of China. "China hasn't looked like this for a long time," I said. "Is this your geography class or your history class?" "Geography," he said. Tiong-chi's father laughed. "In Taiwan," he said, "geography class teaches history, and history class teaches mythology."

Until Lee Teng-hui instigated educational reform in the late 1990s, the Taiwanese educational system taught Chinese geography with maps that appeared to be frozen in time. According to these maps, the People's Republic of China did not even exist, and the Republic of China had the borders of 1911. Even Outer Mongolia, independent since 1911, was included within the boundaries of the Republic of China. The only change was the addition of Taiwan, which did not become part of the Republic of China until 1945. Thus, the maps used in geography class depicted a China that had never existed in political reality. Taiwanese schools were teaching an invented geography as part of the Chinese Nationalist Party's ideological apparatus of social control.

At the same time that schools were teaching ideals of Chinese unity, Taiwan itself was characterized more accurately by ethnic division and unequal development. The Chianan Plain, where I conducted research, remained over 90 percent Holo Taiwanese. The new arrivals from China, now known as Mainlanders, settled mainly in Taipei and in military enclaves in Kaohsiung and Taichung. The Chinese Nationalist state located most of the large infrastructural projects, such as the Hsinchu Science Technological Park, in the north. Southern counties, such as Yunlin, remained relatively poor. Therefore, it is no surprise that when the Chinese Nationalist Party officials reorganized Taiwanese society after 1945, they were perceived by many people in the south as outsiders with limited political legitimacy. The Nationalist state thus had to institute strong measures of social control. The goal of the Chinese Nationalist Party, as explicitly stated in the party charter, is "recovering the Chinese mainland, promoting Chinese culture" (Wachman 1994: 20). To achieve that goal the Chinese Nationalist state needed to convince the island population that the new rulers and the people of Taiwan were equal heirs to a 5,000-year-old Chinese culture. These efforts were neither uncontested nor entirely unsuccessful. Life narratives indeed express a strong identity of "we-Taiwanese" as a nation emerging from colonization, violence, and repression.

MAKING TAIWAN CHINESE

After 1945, the Chinese Nationalist Party quickly embarked on a forced sinicization of Taiwan. The Chinese Nationalists made their physical mark on the island's cities, tearing down Shinto shrines and other Japanese monuments. Japanese-style city districts were replaced with streets named after leaders of the Chinese Nationalist Party, the main concepts of the Three Principles of the People, and place names in China. Tainan Park, originally built by the Japanese, was renamed Sun Yat-sen Park and was endowed with a large statue of the great Chinese Nationalist leader. Statues of Sun Yat-sen and Taiwan's new dictator, Chiang Kai-shek, were erected all over the island. The Chinese Nationalists enshrined Sun Yat-sen as "father of the nation," omitting to mention that Taiwan had not even been part of the Republic of China for the first thirty-four years of its existence.

Until the mid-1990s, even daily activities in Taiwan were couched in nationalistic rhetoric. At large public gatherings such as sports events, graduation ceremonies, musical concerts, and even the shareholders' meetings of large corporations, Taiwanese were expected to stand for the national anthem. Until 1995, they were even expected to do so in cinemas before the showing of a film. Sometimes they even had to bow their heads three times to a picture of Sun Yat-sen. To this day, the year is written as the "-nth" year of the Republic of China, reminding people of the historical foundation of the Chinese nation every time they write the date.

Figure 3.1   The flag of the Republic of China. Some Taiwanese nationalists say it represents only the Chinese Nationalist Party.

In schools, children were taught the Three Principles of the People, an ideology emphasizing nationalism and Chinese identity. Building on the expectation that human identity is oriented "toward the good" (Taylor 1989: 51), these educational campaigns went to great lengths to link this human urge to top-down nationalism. The Three Principles of the People linked the three "modern" values of nationalism, democracy, and people's livelihood[1] with the eight "Confucian" virtues of loyalty and filial piety, charity and benevolence, faith and justice, peace and harmony. Chinese-ness was thus intimately linked to modernity and goodness, and the Chinese were portrayed as the apex of human evolution.

Children were taught their identity as "Chinese" through explicit comparison to foreigners and implicit negation of local differences. For example, at the time of my research, the fifth-grade textbook *Society* described the family life of Westerners as equivalent to that of animals. The text included the following passage:

All mothers and fathers love their own children. That kind of love is instinctive and can be called "primal love." All sub-human animals have that kind of basic instinct. But the "reciprocal love" produced when children perceive their parents' love and return it is not an instinctive characteristic. It is learned through cultural education. In the Western mentality, parents have a responsibility to raise their children and children have a right to be raised. But when the children grow up, they do not have the responsibility of "reciprocal love." (National Institute for Compilation and Translation 1993: 36)

That instinctive form of "primal love" without reciprocity, shared by animals and Westerners alike, was then contrasted to the "Chinese" way of filial piety defined and advocated by Confucius. Westerners were even said to be so ungrateful and heartless that they demanded money for room and board when aged parents came to visit them (National Institute for Compilation and Translation 1993: 39). A photograph of a blue jay feeding its young illustrated the concept of primal love. A photograph of a young Chinese woman sitting on a park bench with an elderly woman illustrated reciprocal love.[2] The chapter concluded with an illustration of a smiling Chinese boy surrounded by his father, his brothers, his friends, his future wife and crowned with a copy of the constitution of the Republic of China.

Most of all, school textbooks demonized the Japanese. The Japanese were depicted as cruel, militaristic barbarians who had enslaved both Korea and Taiwan and inflicted great damage to China. History classes placed great emphasis on the Nanjing Massacre, when Japanese soldiers pillaged, raped, and murdered more than 300,000 people in China in December 1937. Thus, a whole generation of Taiwanese experienced the cognitive dissonance that resulted from conflicting depictions of the Japanese: School lessons taught students that the Japanese were brutal subhumans, whereas their parents shared memories of the Japanese as efficient administrators and kind teachers.

Nationalist education also denigrated local culture, consistently portraying Taiwanese culture as low class (Gates 1981: 253). Folk religious beliefs were more often than not treated as superstitious and backward. Most painfully for the Native Taiwanese, they were forced to learn Mandarin Chinese, the common language of the incoming Mainlanders. Until the 1990s, children were beaten, humiliated, or fined for speaking either Japanese or Taiwanese in school (Morris 2004: 25). In its educational campaigns, the state emphasized that Taiwan was merely one Chinese province among many and that the Chinese Nationalist Party would one day recapture the "mainland." Any discourse that raised the possibility of an independent Taiwan was systematically repressed.

MANUFACTURING CHINESE CULTURE IN HOMES AND WORKPLACES

In its drive to combine national development with Chinese national culture, the Chinese Nationalist state extended its apparatus of social control deep into Taiwanese society. For most adults, development and culture were most strongly reinforced through ideological campaigns in workplaces large and small. Each large factory had a union controlled by Chinese Nationalist Party cadres, and unions often acted in direct collusion with management. Under-cover security forces worked in factories to keep an eye out for potential Communists or advocates of Taiwanese independence from the Republic of China, as well as to weed out potential labor organizers (Arrigo 1985: 86).

Smaller factories, such as the family firms in rural areas, were more diffi-cult to control. Beginning in 1968, as Taiwan entered its export promotion phase of development, the government designed the Community Develop-ment Program to promote home-based industrialization as well as education in ethics and morality. Governor Hsieh Tung-min promoted "Living Rooms as Factories," a campaign to bring the surplus labor of women into industrial production. The government provided loans so that families could purchase machines for small-scale production and then contract with large firms. Cap-italists benefited from the establishment of subcontracting networks, since it enabled them to reduce spending on factory space, energy, dormitories, and food for their workers.

The Living Rooms as Factories campaign included "Mothers' Workshops," which were designed to entice women into the industrial labor force by em-phasizing the traditional role of Chinese wives and mothers as those who

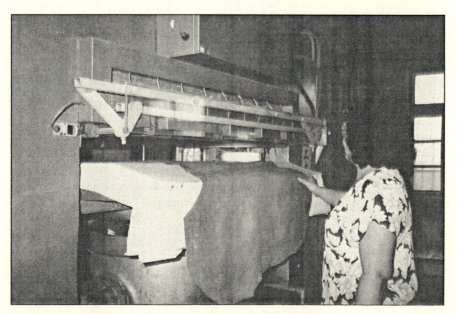

Figure 3.2   A woman working in a Taiwanese leather tannery.

manufacture products at home. Courses focused on Confucian ethics, especially women's contribution to the family economy as faithful wives, devoted mothers, and unpaid workers. Sociologist Ping-Chun Hsiung found that in 1985 and 1986 more than 10,000 participants attended at least 1,000 such classes in Tainan County (Hsiung 1996: 51).

If Confucianism had already been an integral part of daily life in Taiwan, or if its ideology were really more solidly related to industrial production, there probably would have been no need for the Nationalist state to so vigorously promote it as part of their industrialization efforts. Feminist critiques argue that the ideological construction of the "Chinese family firm" in Taiwan was a way of expropriating the labor of women and unmarried men (Greenhalgh 1994; Hsiung 1996). I argue that the discourse also had the ideological goal of transforming the Taiwanese into Chinese. The family, the most intimate sphere of human life, was probably the most effective place for such ideological claims to take root.

FAMILIES AND MARRIAGE IN TAIWAN

The family is by far the most influential institution in Taiwan, just as it is in most societies of the world.[3] The major interconnected patterns of kinship organization in Taiwan include patrilineality, a collective economy with redistribution controlled by one person, division of the family estate among brothers, the formation of a family around a husband and wife within a larger domestic group, and provisions for women's property.[4] Patrilineality, the principle by which surnames and property are passed on through the male line, is still relevant in contemporary Taiwan. With the exception of rare uxorilocal marriages—in which men move into their wives' families—men remain with their own lineage from birth to death.

Property is divided among brothers, usually at the death of their parents. When Taiwan was still a primarily agricultural society, brothers and their families would often remain living together under one roof if warranted by labor needs in agriculture. In spite of a trend toward the nuclear family due to urbanization and industrialization (Marsh 1996; Thornton and Lin 1994), the ties between brothers are still important after marriage. In entrepreneurial families, businesses are often owned and managed by brothers. In a patrilineal system, the lack of a male heir can cause a crisis in the family, as there is no further generation to accept family property as inheritance. Traditionally, the solution has been the uxorilocal marriage, in which a man marries into the family of a woman with no brothers, is accepted as a substitute for a son, and in which the grandchildren take the surname of their mothers.

From a woman's perspective, the family looks very different (Wolf 1972). A woman is said to "marry out" of her natal family and to become a member of her husband's family. A woman is "given" in marriage, whereas a husband "takes" a wife. A woman thus begins married life as a virtual stranger in someone else's household. She has to negotiate a life path between two families, whereas a man is firmly established as a member of one single family from birth to death. Brides, however, are not entirely powerless. Taiwanese women, for example, keep their fathers' surnames at marriage. The bride is also endowed by her parents with a dowry at marriage, and the money stays in her control, becoming the foundation of private savings (Cohen 1976: 188–190). The dowry is perceived as the equivalent of an inheritance, even though its financial value is often much lower.[5]

The family has gone through rapid changes in Taiwan. When anthropologist Myron Cohen conducted his research on Hakka families in southern Taiwan from 1964 to 1965, he could still argue that the family was the main unit of production as well as consumption, although some families were already sending sons into the cities as wage laborers (Cohen 1976). With urbanization and industrialization, however, both men and women earn their own wages autonomously on the labor market. Members of a family no longer necessarily live under the same roof. Many Taiwanese young people leave their homes to seek education and careers in distant Taiwanese cities or even abroad. As a result, holidays are now the best time to observe family life in Taiwan. Holidays have also been influenced by industrialization; improved communications and transportation have made it easier for distant kin to socialize on these occasions (Marsh 1996: 157).

LUNAR NEW YEAR IN TAIWAN

At certain holidays, Taiwanese family members reunite and affirm the kinship ties that bind them. Amidst the banquets, drinking, and gambling of such festive occasions, family members can informally discuss the problems and strategies that the family must face together. Elder family members, for example, warmly encourage junior members to marry and start their own families. In families that combine kinship and entrepreneurship, such events often resemble informal stockholders' meetings, as business is discussed along with family affairs.

Eager to witness firsthand a "Chinese" New Year in Taiwan, I accepted an invitation from a friend to attend a New Year's feast with an entrepreneurial family in Taichung. The events of that evening illustrated to me the structure of Taiwanese families, the ideological underpinnings of that structure, as well as the flexibility of tradition even in the most intimate spheres of family life.

My friend's grandfather, the patriarch of the Ong family, was a well-educated man, having been sent to Tokyo for university during the later years of the Japanese occupation. He married a Taiwanese woman in Japan and raised his three elder children in a crowded six-tatami room in Tokyo. He returned to Taiwan only after the war to pursue a career in teaching. Altogether,

Figure 3.3   New Year's Eve: sharing memories with the younger generation.

he had five sons and two daughters. Now retired, he lives with his eldest son in a small room above his son's sundry goods shop. When I met him for the first time, he was refreshing his Japanese by memorizing the lyrics of Japanese *enka,* a form of folk music popular with older people. While the women cooked downstairs, I talked to the grandfather, pleased to have a chance to practice my Japanese, and he was happy to have an eager listener as he recounted stories of his student days in war-torn Japan.

Downstairs, the storefront had been cleared to make room for a long table and the New Year's banquet. As evening approached, we went downstairs and took our seats surrounded by shelves of socks, women's lingerie, and sundry household goods. The table was loaded with both Taiwanese and Japanese delicacies, including generous portions of sashimi, or raw fish. Four of the five sons and both daughters were present with their families. One son was vacationing in Canada with his wife and children. In jest, they declared that his trip to Canada was a fair exchange, since his seat at the table was taken by an anthropologist from Canada. As we ate, the conversation turned to politics and history, as some of the men related to me the difficulties of the transition from Japanese to Chinese rule, the horror of the February 28 Massacre, and the terrors that Taiwanese intellectuals experienced until the lifting of martial law. Among other things, they were afraid to study Taiwanese local history for fear of being punished as separatists and traitors. I was fascinated and listened attentively. The younger people, however, accustomed to the prosperity and democracy of contemporary Taiwan, were bored with such stories, relegating them to the hazy and not-so-interesting past of their elders.

After dinner, the daughters and their families made an abrupt departure, and from that point on, all activities focused on the patriarchal lineage. My friend's mother, a high school teacher, explained that daughters cannot stay and participate in the events that follow since they have married out and are no longer considered part of the family. Wives spend New Year's Eve with their husband's families, and it is not considered proper for them to pass the evening in their parents' homes. Only sons or unmarried daughters can spend New Year's Eve with their parents. I asked what would happen if the husband's family lived far way, perhaps because the husband had moved to Taipei for a new job, and the wife's family lived nearby. She said the married daughters would still not return to their natal homes and would most likely just stay at home watching the New Year's programs on television. I asked what would happen in the case of a uxorilocal family. She replied that they would celebrate with the daughter's parents because in such a case the married-in man is considered to be their son.

After everyone helped clear the dinner table, the younger family members began their program of entertainment, mostly music and parlor games. The children, ranging in age from grade school to university students, sang songs, played musical instruments, and performed short skits for their elders. At the conclusion of the performances, each unmarried child stood in front of his or her parents, publicly thanking them for the suffering they had endured on their behalf and declaring that they loved them. Then the distribution of gifts began. The grandfather had purchased small gifts, which he distributed to all of the younger people, including college students, in a lottery system. As each child accepted his gift, he bowed to the grandfather and thanked him. The adults then distributed red envelopes, each containing NT$600.[6] The grandfather distributed them first, standing in front of the assembled family members and giving them to the children who waited in line to accept the gift and bow in thanks. In turn, each uncle stood in front of the assembly and distributed red envelopes to all of the young people present.

After midnight, the young family members distributed red candles to everyone present. The eldest grandson first lit the grandfather's candle, and then each person lit his or her candle from that flame. One young college student played the piano while the rest of the family gathered in a circle. Accompanied by the music, each person was expected to stand up and give a speech of thanks and appreciation to the family. The grandfather spoke first, summing up the main events of the family's life in the past year, most notably the death of their grandmother. Then the others spoke, beginning with my friend's mother. She remarked that destiny had brought each one of them into the Ong family and that each woman should feel fortunate to be able to perpetuate the Ong family line. Then the other wives spoke, expressing similar sentiments. The men also stood up to speak, delivering eulogies for their recently deceased mother and expressing appreciation for the suffering their parents had endured in raising them.

As my friend's father spoke, a tear dropped from his eye. In the candlelight, I looked around me and noticed that all of the men were crying. The younger generation spoke next, thanking their parents for providing them with a good education. One young girl who, due to extreme stress over exams, had suffered a nervous breakdown requiring medical intervention that year, thanked her family for their emotional support and broke down into tears. At the end, I was expected to speak. I thanked them for the invitation, remarking that the evening made me realize the debt I have toward my own parents, as well as how much I love them and miss them. Only at three in the morning did we disperse and go home to sleep.

Two days later, the same friend took me to visit a young couple from the Tzu Chi Buddhist Center, a popular lay Buddhist group of which he is a member, and they exchanged stories about how they had passed the New Year. His friends, who had merely eaten dinner and watched television together, inquired curiously about the Ong family festivities. My friend explained to me that the ritual of lighting candles and giving speeches accompanied by piano music had been an idea that he learned from Tzu Chi. He had even purchased the candles and borrowed the piano from that organization. Tzu Chi, he explained, occasionally has a ritual in which the members hold red witnessing candles and, accompanied by piano music, recount what Buddhism has done to improve their lives. Tzu Chi, in turn, had learned that religious ritual from Protestant missionaries.

The events I observed during this New Year celebration taught me important things about Taiwanese society. First, it revealed to me how important the patrilineal family system is to its participants. Having always spent Christmas Eve with my mother's family, I was especially struck by how Taiwanese New Year's festivities are structured by patrilineal ideology. The changing family identities of women as they marry out of their natal families and marry into new families are strongly reinforced on such occasions. The New Year's rituals are not merely a random gathering of kin but clearly define who belongs to which family. The communal feast, the distribution of red envelopes from elder to younger family members, the invitation list which excluded daughters, and even a ritual with its roots in Protestant Christianity reinforced lineage solidarity and defined the places of both men and women within the family.

Second, attendance at this family gathering underscored the way in which contemporary Taiwanese national identity is a hybrid combining elements from Taiwan's colonial past and other interactions with the world. Due to the Japanese past of the family patriarch, they served Japanese food. One grandson introduced a new ritual originally derived from Protestant Christianity. And one son chose to spend his New Year holiday in the Canadian Rockies. Yet all of these foreign elements were incorporated seamlessly into what is often considered to be the most traditional of Chinese holidays. Taiwanese people have long been capable of absorbing foreign elements into even the most intimate spheres of daily life. The family ritual that I observed during this New Year celebration is merely one example of a tradition constantly being reinvented.

RELIGION

In Taiwan, religion extends far beyond formal institutions such as Tzu Chi. Folk religious practices are important to most Taiwanese people and are visibly employed in certain occupations. Construction workers, for example, make sacrifices to the Earth God before beginning work on a project, and they prefer not to work during the seventh month of the lunar calendar, as it is believed that the ghosts of the dead come out from Hell during that time. Almost all Taiwanese business people make food and incense sacrifices to the Earth God on the second and sixteenth days of the lunar month, asking for business success and prosperity. Leather tanners, even in large corporations, are no exception. Most of them have small altars in their offices, and some build small shrines on factory premises. Like other business people, leather tanners believe in *fengshui* or geomancy, the art of manipulating natural energies of the landscape to influence human destiny. They thus design their factories in conjunction with natural features of the landscape to capture prosperity and avoid bad luck.

In one Pingtung tannery, I was told a story about how bad geomancy brought about problems with ghosts. The tannery had a road leading directly to the front gate. According to geomantic principles, that is unfortunate because it can bring misfortune and even ghosts. Shortly after the tannery began production, strange incidents began occurring at night. Workers frequently had accidents, and at night workers reported seeing motorcycles driving themselves around the tannery grounds. The owners thus consulted a spirit medium, who subsequently diagnosed the problem as bad geomancy attracting ghosts from the tombs on the other side of a neighboring coconut grove. In order to correct the problem, they built a small shrine on tannery property and now make monthly sacrifices to appease the ghosts. Since the shrine was erected, no problems with ghosts have been reported. These folk religious beliefs, once used as evidence of Taiwan's Chinese heritage, are now reconstructed as part of Taiwanese identity (Katz 2003).

Figure 3.4   Tannery Shrine.

CIVIL SOCIETY AND SOCIAL MOVEMENTS

Taiwanese people are active in more than their families and religious groups, as Taiwan has a thriving civil society. Especially since the lifting of martial law, social movements have flourished in Taiwan, including those of women, labor, farmers, indigenous peoples, and a variety of environmental and human rights activists (Hsiao 1990; Weller 1999). Many of the tanners are members of the Rotary International and the Lions Club, where they discuss national and international issues at meetings and have exchanges with partners in other countries. Others are active in local party organizations of either the Chinese Nationalist Party or the Democratic Progressive Party. Due to Taiwan's lively media, all of them are aware of the demands of Taiwan's social movements, even beyond the labor and environmental concerns that directly influence their work operations. Like nearly everyone in the south, they listen to "call-in" radio shows in which listeners air their views about such issues as Taiwanese national identity and relations with China. Although individual involvement in civil society varies tremendously in Taiwan, most view it as evidence of a democratic society and have incorporated it into their national identity.

CONCLUSION

The ways in which cultural institutions are labeled are much like the lines on a map. The boundaries are drawn in ways that reflect the interests of the mapmakers and are thus manifestations of power. Maps and cultural institutions alike are taught in school, reproduced through the media, and brought into homes and workplaces through mechanisms of state power. Only in rare cases are they contested as openly as in Taiwan.

Many of the institutions commonly labeled as Chinese, such as the patrilineal family and even New Year's customs, are strong in Taiwan, yet they exist far beyond the shores of Taiwan and even beyond historical China. The patrilineal family is part of a broader Eurasian pattern, including all cultures where children take the surname of their fathers. The lunar New Year is also celebrated on the same day in Vietnam and Korea, where it is labeled respectively as the Vietnamese and the Korean New Year. Confucianism is the basis of cultural identity in Korea, Japan, and Vietnam, as well as in China and Taiwan. The labeling of these institutions as "Chinese" in Taiwan is thus a powerful tool of political hegemony and a product of the social control imposed by the Chinese Nationalist Party.

When I discussed the "Chinese" New Year with some Taiwanese research participants, I was corrected by people who insisted that I call it the "lunar" New Year in order to avoid nationalistic connotations. Relabeling the family, a holiday, or a folk belief as "Vietnamese" or "Taiwanese" or otherwise non-Chinese is likewise an assertion of nationalism, even if the political implications are more obvious in contested Taiwan than in more established nation-states like Vietnam and Japan. These contested national identities further emerge in the remembering of even personal work histories. The next two chapters look at how tanners construct work identities against the backdrop of decolonization and globalization.

Notes

1. A related reading of fraternity, democracy, and equality comes explicitly from the model of the French Revolution.

2. A common critique of this discourse in Taiwan is that it justifies the state providing only limited welfare and pensions to the elderly, on the grounds that their children are responsible for their care.

3. The anthropological classics on the family in Taiwan are Cohen (1976) and Wolf (1968). For women's perspectives on family and marriage, see Wolf (1972), and see Adrian (2003) for contemporary Taipei.

4. It should be noted that these are characteristic of family organization throughout Eurasia (Goody 1990).

5. In the 1990s, feminist lobbying finally led to the passage of inheritance laws stipulating equal inheritance among brothers and sisters. In practice, however, this is not always respected.

6. About US$20 at the time.

CHAPTER FOUR

TANNERS AND FAMILY FIRMS

Seng-li Tannery is one of Taiwan's largest tanneries and was about to become the second tannery listed on the Taipei stock market when I was conducting my research. I wanted desperately to interview the owner, Mr. Tiu, and to learn how he had built up such a large company in a cultural context said to produce small bosses. I went to Seng-li Tannery with Ngo Bi-chu, a friend who had once worked there and claimed she could secure me an interview with the owner. At first, we were stuck sitting in her car at the guardhouse. Only after making several phone calls to Bi-chu's former colleagues inside were we permitted to pass the guardhouse, park the car, and walk up the long, palm tree-lined driveway. On both sides of the lane were flower gardens and even a vast expanse of grass, a rare sight in Taiwan. Next to a parking lot filled with BMWs and Mercedes-Benzes was the office complex, a large pink stucco building. In the back, scarcely visible through the trees, was the tannery itself. The lobby of the office building was no less impressive. The floors were covered with plush carpet, and the walls were decorated with Western art prints.

Seng-li was also one of the few Taiwanese tanneries where I saw managers wear suits and ties to work. My friend asked a middle-aged man in a pinstriped suit and eyeglasses if anyone could help me with my study. After reviewing my questionnaire and consulting with several colleagues, he made his decision. Since none of the managers were members of the Tiu family, he said, they didn't know anything about the Tiu family or their career history. I would have to interview the owner himself. "He has an MBA from Harvard," whispered Bi-chu in my ear. We were escorted down a corridor of offices,

conference rooms, an accounting department, and other offices, all clearly labeled with Plexiglas signs, and were given a seat in a conference room and
served tea.

After approximately twenty minutes, Mr. Tiu, a tall, stocky man of fifty-five,
entered the room surrounded by members of his management team. He asked
to see a list of questions. Prepared for such situations, I gave him my questionnaire, which he read intently. Irate, he declared that my study was of no interest to him at all, especially since questions about family and enterprise were
loaded with outdated "stereotypes about family firms in Taiwan." For example,
he said, I should not ask about the wives of owners, since that question assumes that wives naturally work for their husbands' firms. The questions
about capital are also absurd, he said. The firm didn't get capital from traditional sources like wives' dowries or revolving credit associations, but rather
from bank loans. As for partners, they had hundreds of them and would soon
have many more, as they planned to offer stock on the Taipei stock exchange
in May 1997. "It is racist of you to think we are so backward!" he said in anger.
Nonetheless, he agreed to answer my questions in written form. A few days
later, I received his response along with a brief letter in English. "This questionnaire is only appropriate for Taiwan of thirty years ago," he wrote.

Mr. Tiu was right to point out the implicit dichotomies in my study: tradition versus modernity, family firms versus corporations. His response also
made me conscious of the implications of my cultural assumptions in terms
of identity. By responding to my questions so frankly, he asserted a personal
identity with corporate modernity, which stood in contrast to the aspects of
"Chinese" culture I had been trained to observe. Moreover, he wanted to
teach me that the West had no monopoly on modernity and rationality. Most
importantly, the modernist identity embraced so fervently by Mr. Tiu under-
cut the nationalist discourse of the "Chinese family firm" promoted in the
"Living Rooms as Factories" campaign, labeling that organizational form as
inferior to the corporate firm. At the same time, he asserted that Taiwan was
modern, thus creating an implicit contrast between traditional China and
modern Taiwan. It is not at all uncommon for Taiwanese to perceive themselves as more advanced and more modern than the Chinese.

Nonetheless, scholars generally agree that the economic structure of Taiwan is largely made up of family firms, and the tanning industry is no exception.[1] The first goal of this chapter is to examine both family and corporate
firms in the specific context of the tanning industry to see if there is a domi-
nant pattern. The second goal is to explore the work narratives of the bosses of
family-based firms to see how they identify themselves in terms of modernity
and tradition. Do owners of small, family tanneries identify with Chinese tradition as envisioned by the "Living Rooms as Factories" campaigns? Or is Mr.
Tiu's identification with modernity and corporate organization widespread in
contemporary Taiwan?

DEFINING THE FAMILY FIRM

The first challenge, of course, is to define what constitutes a family firm. Labor participation is not an appropriate definition in Taiwan, because the family is no longer the basic unit of production in Taiwan's manufacturing sector. Less than 3 percent of Taiwan's industrial workers now work for free in factories owned by their families, as wage labor has completely superseded the use of unpaid family labor. By 1991, only 49 of the 10,022 people employed in the industry—less than 0.5 percent—were unpaid family members (DGBAS 1993: 21). Today ownership and management are more appropriate indicators of whether a firm qualifies as a family firm.

Firm Ownership

I define family ownership as firms that are owned exclusively by heads of families (sole proprietorships) or held as kin-based joint ventures. Using this operational definition, valid surveys of tanneries in southern Taiwan show that 47 out of the 68 tanneries (69 percent) are family-owned firms.[2] Of these, 22 tanneries identified themselves as sole proprietorships, sometimes explicitly stating that their families are not involved in their businesses. In most cases, these firms were owned by the family head and managed jointly by him and members of his family. In a few cases, no family members were involved in factory management, with wives and children pursuing their own careers and the factories being run by hired professional management.

Of the 68 tanneries surveyed, 25 identified themselves as joint ventures where the partners were restricted to relatives. Those partners, however, were not necessarily involved in the daily operation of the tanneries. In some of those kin-based joint ventures, the owners proudly noted that they were really sole proprietorships, but they registered relatives as partners because of the lower taxes and limited liability benefits bestowed by the state on limited partnerships. Of the remaining tanneries, 19 were joint ventures with families or firms unrelated to them by kinship, and 2 were listed on the Taipei stock exchange and thus had a multitude of shareholders.[3] Ownership patterns in the industry, based on self-identification in interviews, can be summarized as follows:

Table 4.1   Ownership Patterns in the Taiwanese Tanning Industry

Sole proprietorships	22 (32%)
Kin-based joint ventures	25 (37%)
Non kin-based joint ventures	19 (28%)
Corporations listed on the Taipei stock exchange	2 (3%)

Source: Interviews with tannery owners, 1996–97.

Firm Management

I define family-managed firms as those in which half or more of the management positions are filled by kin. In most of the tanneries surveyed (42 out of 68), at least half of management positions were filled by family members. Out of 42 family-managed tanneries, 35 hired no outside managers at all; 9 of them were run solely by the male household head, 11 were jointly managed by husband and wife, and the remaining 15 were managed by fathers and sons. Only 26 of the firms surveyed were managed primarily by professional management. Management in the industry is organized as follows:

Table 4.2   Management Patterns in the Taiwanese Tanning Industry

Less than 50% of managers are family	26 (38%)
At least 50% of managers are family	42 (62%)

Sources: Interviews with tannery owners, 1996–97.

Relationship Between Ownership and Management

Of the 68 tanneries surveyed, 38 (56 percent) were characterized by both family ownership and family management. Of the 47 firms in which the owners self-identified as sole proprietorships or kin-based joint ventures, 38 were not only owned but also managed primarily by family members. Only 5 sole proprietorships and 4 kin-based family ventures hired professional management and did not classify themselves as family firms when interviewed. Of the 21 tanneries that were not family-owned, 4 were managed primarily by the members of one family, but they were joint ventures with partners unrelated by kinship—a strategy employed primarily to raise capital. The remaining 17 firms were neither family-owned nor family-managed, qualifying them as corporations. The tanneries of southern Taiwan can be categorized as follows:

Table 4.3   Family Ownership and Management

Family-owned and managed	38 (56%)
Family-owned, but professionally-managed	9 (13%)
Dispersed ownership, but family-managed	4 (6%)
Neither family-owned nor family-managed (corporate)	17 (25%)

Sources: Interviews with tannery owners, 1996–97.

Most of the tanneries I studied thus fit the standard representation of "traditional" Chinese family enterprises. Of the total, 69 percent were family-owned, 62 percent were family-managed, and 56 percent were both family-owned and family-managed. These figures need to be placed in perspective, however. The 38 family-owned and family-managed tanneries accounted for only 23 percent of the capital invested in the industry as a whole in southern Taiwan and employed only 34 percent of the tannery workers in the region. The 26 professionally managed firms, on the other hand, accounted for 76 percent of the capital invested and 64 percent of the workers employed in the tanneries of southern Taiwan. The 17 corporate firms accounted for 61 percent of the capital invested and employed 51 percent of the workers in the region's tanneries. Although the majority of tanneries were family-owned and family-managed, the professionally managed firms dominated the industry in terms of both capital investment and labor hiring. This is the larger background against which family firms have been represented as traditionally Chinese and corporations as modern and cosmopolitan. Ethnographical observations and work narratives, however, show that this dichotomy is overstated. Even the owners of family firms assert identities as "modern" and "rational" entrepreneurs within a global context.

SELECTED HISTORIES OF FAMILY TANNERIES

Peikang: A Rural Family Economy

The Peikang District of Yunlin County, one of Taiwan's poorer rural areas, is home to several families that combine tanning with farming activities. By Taiwanese standards, Peikang is a relatively isolated rural district, as it lies neither on the train line nor on the expressway that runs from Taipei to Kaohsiung. The nearest urban center is the small city of Chiayi. Due to the town's relative proximity to Chiayi, most of the Peikang tanneries started out as subcontractors for large tanneries in Chiayi or as suppliers for shoe factories located there.

Of the sixteen leather tanneries in Yunlin County that had registered with the government in 1992, three had already gone out of business by the time I arrived to conduct my research in early 1997. Twelve of the remaining thirteen tanneries were located in Peikang District, six of them in one administrative village. Those six tanneries were scattered about in three dispersed hamlets within the village boundary, and finished hides were laid out in the fields drying in the sun. With no water treatment plants in use, the streams and irrigation canals ran blue with the foul-smelling effluents that flow from the tanneries. Some of the neighbors were obviously displeased with the presence of the polluting industry in their village. One tannery was vandalized, with the characters for "stinky leather" painted across the front of the building.

Most of the tanneries in Yunlin County were small family enterprises. They had an average registered capital of NT$9 million and a median number of fifteen workers. The largest employer in the local tanning industry was a pigskin tannery that relocated to Yunlin from Kaohsiung because they thought that a rural workforce would be less prone to labor disputes. They employed fifty-six production workers.

In terms of ownership, the Yunlin tanneries were all family enterprises, and only one had a partner unrelated to the owner by kinship. In terms of management as well, Yunlin tanners kept business in the family. Only one tannery in the county has employed nonfamily members in management. That tannery was not in rural Peikang, but rather in the relatively urban town of Tounan, located on the railroad. That Tounan tannery, consistently the exception in my analysis of Yunlin tanneries, was also unique because it was owned by a woman, and it recycled leather scraps rather than actually processing raw hides. I discuss the history of this firm in Chapter 6.

Unlike most tanneries in Taiwan, the Yunlin tanneries all used family labor in the production process. In stark contrast to Tainan's Seng-li Tannery, it was difficult for me to distinguish the owners from the workers, as all of them engaged in the labor process directly, working with the hides and tanning chemicals. Eight out of the twelve Peikang wives of owners worked in the tanneries alongside their husbands, and four were housewives uninvolved in the labor process. Like elsewhere in Taiwan, however, they also employed foreign labor. Forty-eight Filipino men and one Filipino woman worked in Yunlin leather tanneries, making up 23 percent of the 216 workers who worked in the local leather industry.

All but two of the Yunlin tannery owners lived and worked in the same place. The exceptions were again the Tounan recycled leather facility and the transplant from Kaohsiung. Eight of the Peikang tanneries were established on inherited agricultural land, distributed to farmers during the period of land reform, and were originally intended to provide only a supplementary income to farming. Two of the tanneries had expanded, purchased land in a small industrial park in Peikang, and owners moved their families into the new tanneries. One tannery had a large professional-looking office, yet the entire staff was composed of family members. Part of the office was even set aside as a nursery for the small children, who were tended by their grandmother.

Peikang was by far the most hospitable place in which I conducted research. In several tanneries, I was invited to stay for meals, joining workers and owners at the large round tables where they ate together every day. One tanner even invited me to join him on a trip to a Chiayi sauna to visit prostitutes, an offer I politely declined. Through these social encounters I discovered that Yunlin tanners were pessimistic about their future and saw no hope of continuing their business into the next generation. With almost the entire shoe industry and many of the tanneries relocating to China and Southeast Asia, it had become increasingly difficult for small rural workshops to survive on subcontracting. Only large firms with international contacts and English-speaking staff had been able to successfully manage relations with shoe facto-

Figure 4.1   The owner of a small tannery at work on the production process.

ries scattered around the Pacific Rim. Unlike tanners in other parts of Taiwan, Peikang tanners had been unable to generate the capital needed for overseas investments. Only one Peikang tanner had managed to invest overseas, and that was a failing joint venture in a Sichuan (China) bowling alley.

As I walked into one tannery, registered with the government as having thirty-four workers and NT$20 million in capital, an old man was leaving the compound in an ox-pulled cart, a rare sight in contemporary Taiwan. I slowly walked past a black ram standing in the doorway and entered the tannery it-self. The tanning drums and other machines were still. No workers were in sight. I slowly backed out when a large dog rushed out from the back room and began barking fiercely at me. A man walked out of the house and asked me whom I was looking for. When I told him that I was doing a study of the Taiwanese leather industry, he took me into the house, offered me a seat and a cup of tea, and went upstairs to find Chiu Bing-jin, the owner. Saying he had nothing else to do, he shared with me his life history and showed me around the tannery, emphasizing how pitiful his life had become now that business had dried up almost entirely.

Mr. Chiu was born in 1948 in Yunlin. After he graduated from primary school he went to Chiayi to work in a leather tannery there. At the time, he said, there were many shoe factories and tanneries in Taiwan, and workers were willing to work twelve or even sixteen hours a day for a pittance of a salary. Like many others of his generation, he saved his wages and eventually built his own tannery on his family's farm.

Ten years ago, business was thriving. He invested NT$20 million in the tannery and once employed thirty-four workers. But with high wages, rising prices of raw materials, and the loss of important customers when large tanneries and shoe factories left Taiwan, his business had foundered. His tannery now had only five workers, including himself and two sons who did most of the work. "When there is any work at all to be done," he added sadly.

Mr. Chiu gave me a tour of the factory. Many parts of the tannery were now empty, the machines having been sold off to meet pressing financial needs. Most machines were silent, but one tanning drum started slowly revolving as we toured the plant. Some machines were covered entirely in dust, and the drying rack was being used to dry the family's laundry rather than hides. His son and two workers were pushing leather through the splitting machine. He said they had so few orders that they could no longer afford to run the entire production process at once. Instead, his sons and two hired workers slowly put the hides through the entire process step by step themselves.

Mr. Chiu took me upstairs and showed me a large empty office. He once employed three secretaries, he said, but now they didn't even use the office. The telephones had been removed. FAX and telex machines were covered with dust. He showed me a stack of unused invoice forms, printed for the company but never used because the orders dried up. A display room designed to exhibit leather samples was now just a playroom for his children, a place to watch TV and play mahjong. Behind the office, there was a dormitory, a kitchen, and a recreation room with a billiard table. They had formerly been used by Thai workers, he said, but were now abandoned. Tanning was a "sunset industry," he explained, since the shoe factories had moved overseas.

Peikang, however, is only one part of the leather tanning industry. Some family firms, primarily in Kaohsiung and Tainan, have adapted well to the globalization of the industry. Their integration into global networks, as well as the ways in which they highlight immigration experiences in their narratives, asserts an identity that is global, modern, and yet still very Taiwanese.

Somerset Leather: A Successful Family Tannery
Kaohsiung's Liong-hong Tannery, which uses the British-sounding name of Somerset Leather in foreign trade, stood in stark contrast to the impoverished family tanneries of Peikang. The factory was surrounded by a neatly maintained brick wall with a sparkling white entrance gate, and the name of the factory was written in both English and Chinese. A brand-new pagoda in Chinese architectural style had been erected on top of the parking garage. Inside the gates was a meticulously landscaped garden. Two large iron cages that looked like they belonged in a Victorian zoo adorned the office building

in the center of the courtyard. One was full of peacocks, and the other contained menacing-looking dogs, which were used at night to patrol the factory grounds.

I went into the office, where four women in crisp blue uniforms were working at their desks. Golf trophies adorned the office, as well as certificates of registration with the government, a faded image of Sun Yat-sen, and a photo of the tannery's owner posing with President Lee Teng-hui. On the walls hung wooden signboards, carved with the Chinese characters for prosperity and wealth, which had been given to them by well-wishing business partners. There were several wall calendars with maps of the United States on them, given to them by American hide companies, a rack of baseball glove samples, and the usual clutter of computers, fax machines, and photocopy machines. I told them about my project and was given permission to interview Ong Bi-le, the owner's unmarried daughter, who spoke English and handled the firm's import and export affairs.

I started out the interview by asking her about her family's history. They owned the leather tannery, a baseball glove factory in Taiwan, and another baseball glove factory in the Philippines. The tannery had been started by Ong Cheng-bu, her grandfather. During the Japanese occupation of Taiwan, he received a Japanese education, becoming fluent in both written and spoken Japanese. As a young man, he went to work in a Japanese chemical factory and learned how to work with the chemicals used in tanning.

After several years of experience, he was sent to Hainan Island, off the southern coast of Guangdong Province in China, where he worked in management for a Japanese-run tannery. After the war, he came back to Taiwan and started his own tannery. As the tannery grew more profitable, the business expanded, and then began manufacturing baseball gloves.

The company was a good example of a successful family tannery, since all of the male relatives and their wives worked together in the company. Her grandfather had had seven children. The four daughters all married out of the family, and all three sons stayed with the family to work in the tannery. The eldest son was her father. Since the grandfather no longer worked in the tannery, he had taken over as president and CEO. His wife was the financial manager of the tannery.

The second son was in charge of the baseball glove factory in the Philippines. His wife, who had worked in the baseball glove factory in Taiwan, retired from the company when they moved to the Philippines. "Salaries are so low there," explained Bi-le, "that she doesn't have to work. They can hire Filipino people to do all the work." The third son was the general manager of the tannery, and his wife was the production manager of their Taiwanese baseball glove factory.

The third generation, however, was less involved in tannery affairs. Only the three children of the elder son had reached adult age. The elder son was working on his Ph.D. in electrical engineering in California. He had a family in the United States and had already acquired permanent residency there. He planned to return to Taiwan upon completion of his studies, but he did not want to work in the tannery. The younger son was still working on his bachelor degree in economics in the United States and was likely to return to work in the tannery. Their daughter, whom I interviewed, had already graduated from a California university and had returned to the tannery, where she planned to work until marriage. Their story illustrates how family firms can prosper by finding their own niche in a globalizing economy.

Kok-eng Tannery: Family Division

The Taiwanese are well aware of the problems that can emerge in families and family enterprises, and several well-known proverbs point out those problems. "Wealth does not exceed three generations," says one commonly quoted proverb, reflecting the tendency of families to divide their wealth among heirs and thereby lose it. "Every family has a scripture that's hard to recite" uses Buddhist imagery to suggest that every family has stress and problems. Actual work relations at Somerset are probably not as harmonious as they appear to the outside world, but at least they have managed to stay together. Neighboring Kok-eng Tannery, on the other hand, is an example of a wealthy family tannery that did not manage to stay together.

Sim Kok-eng was born in Kaohsiung County in 1914. Like many others of his generation, he started leather tanning by working in one of the tanneries established by the Japanese. Mastering the technology quickly, he became one of their leading technicians. He was sent to Hainan Island, where he worked with Ong Cheng-bu, the founder of Somerset Leather. They became close friends and sworn brothers. When the Japanese lost the war in 1945, the two men came back to Taiwan. Ong Cheng-bu opened up Somerset Leather tannery, and Sim Kok-eng went to work there as a technician. As soon as he acquired enough capital, however, he left. Using both his own savings and money contributed from his parents, he opened up his own tannery just down the street from Somerset.

In the early days, their tannery was a typical family enterprise, with the husband managing the factory and the wife in charge of sales. They had four sons and two daughters. Now in the second generation, the tannery had expanded, and the family manufactured a wide range of leather and leather products. In total, they owned two leather tanneries in Taiwan, one tannery in Shanghai, several shoe factories in Taiwan and China, as well as a construction company in Taiwan. After the father's death, the elder son, Sim Ching-bun, took over management of the tannery in Kaohsiung.

The second son had studied electronics and then pursued a career in management at an electronics firm. Sim Ching-kok, the third son, chose an entirely different career path. He earned an M.A. in Chinese from a university in Taipei and then returned to Tainan to teach at Cheng Kung University. However, after a few years, his father asked him to return to the family company, and he took a job managing one of the family shoe factories. In 1980, he had a disagreement with his elder brother and left Kaohsiung. He then bought a leather factory that came up for sale in neighboring Tainan County and now was the president and CEO. That purchase and subsequent move was described by the son as a "family division." His younger brother and younger brother-in-law both worked with him in management. This company had been very successful. Although it employed only forty workers, the company also operated tanning facilities in Shanghai. In order to accommodate the rapid growth of their company, they shifted from family to professional management, hiring five of their eight upper-level managers from outside the family.

Since the purchase of the tannery in Tainan County, the original tannery in Kaohsiung had also expanded. In 1987, they moved from their original location in their home village to an industrial park just outside of town, where they now employed seventy workers. The management of this company still remained entirely in family hands. Sim Ching-bun, the founder's eldest son, was now the president, and his wife worked in labor management. His younger brother was the general manager. A paternal cousin was the production manager, and Sim Ching-bun's son was in charge of sales. A nephew and daughter-in-law worked in the lower ranks of management.

The father explained that their family continued to prosper because they did not divide up legal ownership of the companies and they continued to pool capital. Management and operation of the tanneries, however, had been divided, and the two brothers did not cooperate. This arrangement allowed both brothers the autonomy they sought, but forestalled a complete division of the firm. A complex shareholding system separated ownership from management and preserved collective family ownership in spite of separate management. Both tanneries were shareholding corporations, and the brothers owned stock in both companies. The shoe companies were also legally separate entities, and they all owned stock in those companies as well. These were all strategies of managing conflicts within the family businesses.

FAMILY TIES: KEEPING GOOD MANAGEMENT

In spite of the problems encountered by family firms, some tanneries prefer to hire family rather than professional managers. In interviews, most of them described their kin-based hiring practices in terms of business needs rather than cultural practices, thus exhibiting an identity in concert with professional and global norms of rational management. Many tanners said, for example, that professional managers were likely to leave if they received a more attractive job offer from a competing tannery. Family members were constrained to a certain extent by an ideology that stressed family loyalty, a pressure that made it more difficult to leave and join the competition. If adequate labor resources were available in the family, giving management positions to family members was a rational strategy to reduce the risk of losing valuable management talent.

Bat-lim Leather in Tainan County, for example, is a recently established family-managed tannery. When I visited this factory unannounced one February afternoon, I was warmly received by Iu Chi-bun, the company's owner. He served me tea and answered my questions in detail, offering me detailed information about his personal history and the establishment of his tannery. After graduation from high school, he said, he studied chemistry for two years at a technical institute in Tainan. He expected to join the army but was refused by the military on the grounds that he was too short, and thus he was free to concentrate on his career at a young age. His chemistry teacher got him a job as a chemical technician at Formosa Leather, where the president was the teacher's brother-in-law. He worked there for five years, before taking a higher-paying job at Tai-hoa, another corporate tannery. He spent eleven years there but eventually left when he was offered a more lucrative position as factory manager at another tannery. He stayed there for only two years before leaving to open his own tannery. Constructed in 1991, Bat-lim Tannery had become one of the largest tanneries in Taiwan by 1997, employing more than one hundred workers.

Due to high entry costs, it is no longer feasible for most families to enter tanning with only their own resources. In terms of ownership, Bat-lim Tannery was thus not a stereotypical family tannery but a rather complex joint venture. With an initial investment of NT$20 million (US$635,000), Iu Chi-bun bought land and built a factory in a small village north of Tainan. The start-up capital was a mix of his own savings, bank loans, and venture capital from thirty-three stockholders, only five of whom are kin. Other partners include former classmates, colleagues from the other tanneries where he had worked, technicians who worked in the tannery, and corporate investors in related leather goods and chemical industries. Eventually, they planned to offer stocks for public sale. Mr. Iu was modest about his company's achievements: "We started small, with only thirty-four workers. Every year, I reinvested the profits and we grew slowly from year to year. Now it's a big factory with over one hundred employees. You can't just start up with a big factory like this."

Mr. Iu said that his tannery was "unusual" because all of the important management positions were held by family members. In addition to himself as president, his wife was the financial manager, his wife's elder brother was the general manager, and his wife's younger brother was the production manager. Two nephews, sons of his elder brother and elder sister, and the husband of one of his nieces, filled the lower ranks of management. His own son had just completed military service and was studying English in preparation for attending school at a leather tanning institute in England. He planned to come back and work in the tannery after graduation.

I asked him why the company staffed management positions with only family members, instead of hiring professional management, like most other large tanneries. "Because it's a new factory," he replied. "We don't want to hire nonfamily management, because if you find good people, there is a risk that they will leave to join another factory." He stressed the difficulties of setting up a leather tannery. It is already difficult to acquire investment capital, technology, and a customer base. Most difficult of all, however, is human capital. In order to survive in a competitive market, tanneries need to get skilled laborers and good managers and keep them in the firm. As his career demonstrated, the most skilled managers are likely to leave if they get more lucrative job offers from other tanneries; this mobility only helps the competing firms. As a new company, he could not afford to lose good talent. Instead of hiring professional managers, he cultivated talent from among his own relatives, firmly believing that family loyalty would keep them in his firm. Nonetheless, he reinforced family ties with high salaries and partial ownership in the tannery.

Oan-tong Leather in Tainan County went even further. Like Bat-lim Tannery, all management positions were held by relatives. Moreover, the four brothers who owned the tannery all worked directly in the labor process as technicians, each of them supervising a different part of the labor process. Mr. Su, the president, said that only family firms such as his can guarantee consistently high quality, because they can rely on family members to stay in the firm as technicians. It takes three to five months for a new technician to adjust to the conditions in a new tannery. Even if he has years of experience elsewhere, each tannery is different. Water in different places, he explained, can vary greatly in terms of temperature and pH levels even within the same county. Technicians thus need to learn from experience how the water in a particular location will react with tanning chemicals and hides. During that learning period, even the best technicians cannot provide the best-quality leather. Bureaucratic firms cannot guarantee good quality, because the high labor mobility of technicians and the constant need to train new people influences the quality of their goods. Family firms like his, stressed Mr. Su, can survive because they produce the high-quality leather that only experienced technicians can provide.

DISCUSSION

The work narratives of tanners and their family members in even the smallest tanneries reveal some interesting dynamics of identity. I had entered the field expecting tanners and their families to assert a Chinese identity through their work narratives, since Chinese identity was so strongly promoted in the "Living Rooms as Factories" campaign and because small-scale entrepreneurs are identified as products of Chinese culture in much of the scholarly literature. Mr. Chhoa and other Taiwanese nationalists had prepared me for resistance to that discourse. Nonetheless, I found that identity could not be easily characterized as either Chinese or Taiwanese. If anything, they sidestepped national issues by describing their business practices in terms of rational management norms.

The kin strategies of the smaller entrepreneurs are clearly shaped by cultural patterns usually labeled as Chinese, but that could also be seen as Taiwanese. At the same time, many tanners revealed other important dimensions of their identities: as entrepreneurs and craftsmen trained by the Japanese, as immigrants to the United States, as investors in China and Southeast Asia, and as employers of Southeast Asian workers. They frequently positioned themselves not in greater national narratives but in relation to professional identities and rational business practices.

At the end of an evening in one of the smallest tanneries in Yunlin, I asked the owner to identify the strongest influences of Chinese culture in his business practices. He responded by asking where I got the idea that there was any connection between the two. "In books," I said. "Many scholars say that Chinese culture has influenced entrepreneurs. . . ." He interrupted to ask whether the authors were Chinese or foreign. When I said I was referring to the Chinese-language literature, he burst into laughter, saying, "Those scholars sure know how to brag about nothing!" He then offered this insight:

> The Chinese have been making leather for thousands of years, but it has just been enough to cover their own bodies. Taiwan has a modern tanning industry only because of foreign technology. The industry was started by the Japanese, the chemicals come from Germany, the machines come from Italy, and the workers come from Thailand. Leather tanning has nothing to do with Chinese culture.

With this reply, he linked his business identity with technological forms of global production. If even the smallest entrepreneurs are so cosmopolitan, it should come as no surprise that the owners of larger corporations assert a global modernity as well. They are the subjects of the following chapter.

Notes

1. This characteristic is by no means unique to Taiwan. The Italian (Blim 1990) and even Canadian economies, for example, are also dominated by small family firms.

2. In the discussion in this chapter, I eliminate the two firms who refused to answer questions about ownership and management.

3. Listing on the stock exchange by no means indicates that they are not family firms. In the next chapter, I take a closer look at these two firms and how their leading families maintain control of the firms by majority shareholding.

CHAPTER FIVE

CORPORATE AND FIRM NETWORKS

Beginning in the 1980s, Taiwan began a process of economic liberalization that altered the conditions for small businesses. Private investors were slowly allowed to enter into industries such as banking that were once dominated by the state. In a concentrated effort to rationalize the private sector, the state also encouraged small private firms to expand and adopt corporate forms of organization. When firms register as share-issuing corporations, for example, they reap the benefits of lower tax rates and limited legal and financial liability. Sociological studies of Taiwanese business groups show that liberalization of financial industries and capital markets from 1987 to 1993 accelerated a move from family to corporate forms of ownership and management (Chung 2004). The tanners I met during field research often emphasized this point.

GENERAL TENDENCIES IN THE TAIWANESE TANNING INDUSTRY

Leather tanners identify two major trends in leather tanning, reflecting changes in the Taiwanese economy in general. The first is a trend toward corporate organization, meaning a separation of ownership and management and the increased hiring of professional managers. The second is a shift away from labor-intensive to capital-intensive production. By the time I did my research, 78 percent of leather processing firms were registered as legal corporations, the remaining 22 percent being noncorporate entities of the sole proprietorship or joint venture types (DGBAS 1993: 292).

In tanning, the trend toward corporatization means that capital investment is now as important as skills in opening up a tannery. In southern Taiwan, in fact, sixteen out of sixty-eight (24 percent) tanneries were started by individual investors with absolutely no experience in tanning at all. Of those tannery owners with related professional experience, twenty-six (38 percent) had worked on the production line. Twelve individuals (18 percent) had worked in tannery management. Six (9 percent) had worked in management in related industries such as shoe companies. Four (6 percent) had been involved in hide or leather trade. Only nine individuals (13 percent) had learned tanning and business skills from working for their own family's tanneries.[1] The narratives of these entrepreneurs thus reveal professional identities ranging from nimble investors to skillful craftsmen.

Once they start tanneries, Taiwanese tanners are not reluctant to hire talented nonfamily professionals to fill management positions. In fact, 74 percent of the individuals employed in the industry's managerial ranks are not related to their employers. This is the most direct evidence of a trend toward separation of ownership and management in the industry. Most tanners say it is necessary to hire management talent on the labor market because it is rarely possible to find all of the skills a factory needs within the family and friendship circles of the owner.

Tanners with capital but no skills must hire everyone from technicians to management from other tanneries, since neither they nor their family members know anything about the craft. Such tanners complain about high mobility among managers and technicians. Competing tanneries often raid the management ranks of their peers with offers of higher salaries to win the most talented managers into their ranks. In order to gain the loyalty of skilled managers, some large companies have thus begun issuing shares in the company to high-ranking managers, a practice also common in North America.

FROM TEETH TO SKINS: A CAPITALIST TANNERY

Sixteen of the tanneries I studied were started by enterprising individuals who saw leather as a profitable business and decided to invest in the field. With no experience at all in tanning, they bought existing tanneries and hired professional tanners to manage the production process. Tainan County's Gak-heng Tannery is just one example of such a capitalist tannery. In this factory, I interviewed Tan Bun-seng, the assistant general manager. Looking over my factory list, he noted that there were now very few family factories left in Taiwan. The major players—Tai-hoa, Seng-li, and Kiu-cheng—were all professionally managed corporations.

Gak-heng itself is a relatively new tannery. It was started in 1979, when Taiwan's shoe industry was in rapid expansion. Li Ling-bing, the owner, was born into a well-established capitalist family. His father, the owner of a processed food factory, had seven children, most of whom did not continue to work in the food industry. The eldest son left and opened up an electronics factory. The second child, a daughter, married out. The second son became a medical doctor and now teaches at Kaohsiung Medical College. The third son took over the family's food processing company. The two younger brothers are both medical doctors. They operate a clinic together, and one teaches at Kaohsiung Medical College. The fourth son went to dental school. Unsatisfied with dentistry, however, he turned to his family to find a job. He first worked for the family's food processing company and then at his brother's electronics factory. In addition to his own salary, he also earned dividends from an investment in An-ping Tannery (see below). After accumulating enough seed capital and securing a bank loan, he bought his own tannery, a bankrupt company that came up for sale. With little knowledge about tanning or leather, he had to rely entirely on hired management and technicians.

Proud of his individual initiative, Mr. Li stressed to me that his family had never been involved in the tannery in any way. His three children have college educations and show no interest in working for their father's firm. Rather than expecting them to take over the tannery, their father encourages them to pursue their own career interests. This lack of family involvement means that he has to run the tannery with hired labor and management. He hires eighty-nine workers, six managers, and five "office ladies,"[2] none of whom have any kin relation to him. This tannery is thus a good example of a sole proprietorship, owned by an individual who does not run the company with family labor.

These professional identities as individualistic, risk-taking entrepreneurs are reinforced through dense social networks based on common occupation, as well as through professional competition with other tanneries. In their career narratives, tanners thus draw a careful distinction between members of their trade, called *lai-hang,* or trade insiders, and *goa-hang,* or trade outsiders. The strongest praise tanners could give me when I exhibited some knowledge of the production process was to say *"li chin lai-hang"* ("You are a real insider"). By working together as laborers on the same factory floor, or through sustained contact as in the case of a raw hide agent and a tannery owner, ties of trust can develop between individuals in the trade that can later be drawn upon for mutual benefit. These social ties lead to the development of what tanners call "friends in the same profession" *(tong-hang peng-iu).* These social ties take business far beyond the family sphere.

AN-PING LEATHER:
A PROFESSIONALLY RUN JOINT VENTURE

One sunny afternoon in May, I met Ang Chi-hui, now a hide trader, in his office near Tainan's Cheng Kung University. He told me the story of An-ping Leather, one of Taiwan's most famous joint venture tanneries. Mr. Ang himself was once president of An-ping. He is Taiwanese, born in Tainan in 1934, and a graduate of the Chemical Engineering Department at Cheng Kung University. He had his first experience in tanning at Formosa Leather, the older tannery described in Chapter 2, when he took a summer job there as a technician, although he never intended to go into leather: "I still don't know why I did tanning. We just happened to live next door to the owner of Formosa Leather, and he was my elder brother's friend. I helped them out in the summers while I was in college, and then I just stayed on after graduation."

Upon graduation from university, he began working full-time at the tannery and quickly rose to the position of production manager, a post he held from 1956 to 1969. Formosa Leather treated him well, giving him on-the-job training as well as sending him abroad to study leather tanning. He spent six months at a leather institute in Germany and another six months studying leather technology in Japan. Since he is proficient in Japanese, German, and English, he has been instrumental in bringing advanced leather tanning techniques to Taiwan, translating leather research reports for Formosa Leather.

In 1969, he and several colleagues left Formosa Leather to start their own leather company. "Back then," he said, "everyone wanted to be his own boss. It wasn't like now, when everyone prefers to work for someone else." They started out with eight partners. He himself was a technician, in charge of production, while the others took care of marketing. Some of the partners were known as "leather leaders," middlemen who sold leather to shoe factories, handbag factories, belt factories, and other leather goods producers. Of the eight partners, four were former employees of Formosa Leather, and two were leather leaders. Two were *tong-hang* "friends" from other tanneries, who only contributed capital. Each of the eight partners contributed NT$500,000, for a total investment of NT$4,000,000. In 1969, that was enough to buy land and construct a factory. With the land and factory as collateral, they were able to secure a bank loan to buy equipment. They located the tannery near a major highway, so that transportation would be convenient, and specialized in cow upper leather.

Since professionalism remains central to his work identity, Ang Chi-hui emphasized that he has always kept tanning separate from his family life. His wife is a high school teacher, and neither she nor their children have any interest in tanning. His daughter has a Ph.D. and is a college professor in Taichung. His son has an M.S. from an American university and is now running his own business in Internet technology.

I asked him if it was difficult to avoid conflicts among non-kin partners in a joint venture. He said no, that relations among them were very good because they defined their jobs very distinctly. More important, he said, they made a profit every year. An-ping Tannery was so successful, and its management spun off so many bosses, that it has come to be called "Leather University." Three big tanneries have split off from An-ping: Tai-hoa, Gak-heng, and Kiu-cheng. Tanners still refer to them as An-ping's children.

In 1991, changes in the wider Taiwanese political economy led to the closure of An-ping, still a profitable tannery at the time. The main problem, argued Ang, was the introduction of the Labor Standards Law. Tanneries were having trouble finding labor as it was, but with the introduction of that law, government regulations became more onerous, and they had to pay a lot for welfare benefits. Second, the area around the factory had become urbanized. Neighbors were complaining because of the smell and water pollution. With rapid urbanization, land prices rose, and they calculated that the profit from the sale of the land would be even higher than what they were earning from leather production. Furthermore, Tai-hoa, a large tannery started by one of their former managers, had already "grown up," and the competition was cutting into their profits. In 1994, only three years after An-ping closed its doors, Taiwan instituted a new system of hiring foreign labor in order to address the island's labor shortage. If the system had been in place earlier, mused Ang, An-ping might not have closed.

SEN-HOA TANNERY:
AN ANTI-POLLUTION COALITION

Sen-hoa Tannery, located next door to a pig farm in rural Tainan County, is a unique joint venture set up by a coalition of Taiwanese leather tanners. Arriving at the tannery on a hot day in the spring of 1997, I noticed immediately that the tannery was different from others I had visited. The first clue was that the unpleasant odors were even stronger than usual, and the tannery courtyard was swarming with flies. Unlike many tanneries, there were no women trimming leather in front of the manufacturing area, and I saw no piles of leather scraps about to be shipped out for recycling. Instead, there was an open building filled with the largest collection of raw hides I had ever seen.

Mr. Iu, the manager with whom I had an interview, led me into the building and we took our seats in the company's conference room. A secretary brought us cartons of iced wheat tea, and we began our interview. Mr. Iu emphasized from the beginning that Sen-hoa Tannery was a special case, especially since it had never been a family tannery. Instead, it was a joint venture started by a group of investors in order to solve a common problem faced by leather tanneries. Leather is tanned in the two stages of wet and dry tanning (see Appendix II). Wet tanning uses a chrome-based chemical process to transform raw animal hides into "wet-blue" hides that resist decay. Dry tanning transforms wet-blue hides according to customer specifications into sheets of leather that can be manipulated into shoes, belts, and other leather products. Since the wet tanning process is heavily polluting and smelly, tanneries face increasing opposition from their neighbors. In the face of such opposition, some tanneries have stopped doing wet tanning and have shifted to dry tanning. Some tanneries merely purchase wet-blue hides from domestic or foreign suppliers; others have moved their wet tanning facilities outside of Taiwan to places such as China or the United States.

Sen-hoa Tannery, as a domestic tannery that specializes in wet tanning, is an important part of this new division of labor. In the 1980s, a raw hide trader named Mr. Ng noticed that tanneries were importing increasing numbers of wet-blue hides rather than raw hides, yet they lacked a reliable supplier. Forming a coalition of raw hide suppliers, *tong-hang* acquaintances, and tanners, he bought out a struggling tannery in 1987. He cut out the dry tanning operations and specialized only in wet tanning, producing a secure supply of wet-blue hides for his partners and other customers. By 1997, the tannery's thirty workers were producing 2,000 hides a day, which were eagerly bought up by most of the tanneries in Taiwan. The tannery's remote location next to an already smelly pig farm has so far allowed it to avoid neighbors' protests, and its combined capital resources have permitted it to build water treatment facilities that meet government environmental standards. When the government strengthens and enforces environmental protection laws, said Mr. Iu, their business can only improve.

From the very beginning, Sen-hoa Tannery has never been identified with any one family. Even family enterprises that adopt corporate management practices often remain family-owned, with one family controlling at least 50 percent of the company's shares. At Sen-hoa Tannery, however, Mr. Ng and nine unrelated partners all have equal shares in the company. Although the identity of these partners is a company secret, Mr. Iu said that some of them are Taiwan's leading tanners. They invest in Sen-hoa as a stable subcontractor that can meet their needs for wet-blue hides.

As a corporation rather than a family firm, Sen-hoa Tannery relies on nonfamily professionals to carry out management tasks, and Mr. Iu himself is one example. He studied printing in school. After the completion of his military service, he went into leather, working at An-ping, a joint venture tannery in which his elder sister's husband was a partner. That brother-in-law, the dentist described above, eventually sold out his shares in An-ping and opened up his own tannery. Mr. Iu worked there for several years, but then took a job in China as a consultant for a Taiwanese company opening up a tannery there. In 1996, he gained a salary increase, a new title, and a chance to return to Taiwan by taking a job as general manager at Sen-hoa.

I asked him if the president had any relatives working in the tannery. He said that the president had a nephew working on the production line as a tannery worker. I said I was surprised that a relative of the president would take such a hard job, since it is rare for family members to work directly in leather production. The nephew just started working there, he explained, and they chose to start him in production to teach him about the industry. I asked if they planned to promote him into management. He merely laughed, saying, "That would depend on his ability, and he doesn't seem to have much. I think he will get tired of the difficult work and leave." His retelling of this story reinforced his identity as manager of a modern, rationally managed corporation.

TANNERIES ON THE STOCK MARKET

Perhaps the largest step that a firm can take away from the family form is to open up ownership to complete strangers by issuing stock in the company and raising capital on the open market. Ever since the Taipei Stock Exchange was established in 1962, Taiwanese firms have increasingly looked to capital markets. In the leather industry, two tanneries are traded publicly on the Taipei stock market. Since these companies are required to publish annual reports to stockholders, their operations are more transparent than most companies. The following analysis is based on both interviews and data from annual reports.

Hong-soa Tannery, with its corporate headquarters in Kaohsiung and its tannery in Tainan County, is the world's largest pigskin tannery. The company was established in 1980 by Tan Chi-seng, who saw in leather tanning a profitable way to recycle the pig hides cast away by Taiwanese slaughterhouses. With an initial investment of NT$10 million, he registered his new corporation and began preparations to build the factory. Two years later, he purchased land in Tainan County, not far from Formosa Leather. In 1987, after a water treatment plant had been installed, Tan registered his factory with the government and began production. He declared the value of his company at NT$29 million. The company has consistently been at the forefront of Asian leather tanning, being the first tannery in Asia to purchase automated drying machinery and to set up full recycling and water treatment facilities. According to government registration records, Hong-soa had a registered capital of NT$600 million in 1992 and employed 255 workers. In 1993, they posted an after-tax income of NT$114,962,000 (US$3,650,000), enabling them to distribute a respectable dividend of NT$1.92 per share to each stockholder.

In spite of its listing on the stock market and its polished corporate image, Hong-soa still maintained many of the characteristics of a family enterprise. Tan Chi-seng, the owner and CEO, controlled 18.8 percent of the company's stock. His wife did not work in the company, but 9.7 percent of the firm's stock was listed in her name. Tan Chiu-sun, the oldest son, owned 31.05 percent of the stock. One of his sons, Tan Chiu-iu, was general manager and owned another 18.9 percent of the company's stock. Another son, Tan Chiu-chun, was the assistant manager in charge of domestic marketing and owned 3.5 percent of the stock. The daughter Tan So-iung was also an assistant manager, in charge of the company's financial department. She owned 1.3 percent of the company's stock. Tan So-iung's husband was assistant general manager and owned 0.1 percent of the company's stock. Another daughter owned 1.24 percent of the company. Together the immediate family controlled 84.59 percent of the company's stock and occupied nearly all of the company's key management positions. The experience of Hong-soa shows that familism is not necessarily incompatible with corporate organization, stock markets, or large profits.[3]

Seng-li Tannery, whose owner Mr. Tiu had taken offense at my questions on traditional culture (see Chapter 4), is practically the ideal of corporate capitalism and modernist ideology. In addition to the questionnaire he returned, I also gained access to a four-hundred-page report made public at the time of their initial public stock offering and gained information from other tanners about his firm. One of the most highly educated tanners in Taiwan, Mr. Tiu finished university before going to work at Formosa Leather, owned by one of his paternal uncles. After gaining experience and saving enough capital of his own, he left Formosa Leather and opened up a baseball glove factory. In 1973, at the age of twenty-nine, he expanded into leather tanning, with an initial investment of NT$8,000,000. Seng-li has consistently been a leader in technological innovation, water treatment, and even the recycling of waste materials from the tanning process. In 1993, for example, Seng-li built a factory to recycle waste materials from all of southern Taiwan's leather tanneries and has been converting tanning sludge into fertilizer. By 1996, Seng-li reported an after-tax net profit of NT$447,520,000 and increased its registered capital to NT$3,630,000,000.

Seng-li Tannery fit the ideal type of a modern corporation with professional management and dispersed ownership, comparable to North American corporations. Tiu and two brothers sat on the board of directors of the company. Together, however, they owned only about 25 percent of the company's stock, and their wives held only 0.14 percent each, a stark contrast to Hong-soa, which concentrated stock in family hands. Management was primarily in the hands of professional talent, with hiring based on skills and experience rather than kinship ties. Of the top eleven managers in the company, only one (one of the three brothers) was within two kinship grades of the owner. One of the four vice presidents was even recruited from Japan to work at Seng-li.

These two firms, as with any group of publicly listed corporations, reveal two important things about Taiwanese industry. First, the very existence of the Taipei Stock Exchange and the willingness of firms to raise capital on the stock market show that there is no cultural obstacle to corporate formation in Taiwan. Second, being listed on the stock market does not necessarily mean that the company is not a family enterprise. Publicly traded tanneries such as Hong-soa still maintain majority family ownership and control of their firms. Other firms, such as Seng-li, are able to corporatize completely, accepting a majority of both capital and skills from outside the family.

Over the course of my research, I visited many different kinds of leather tanneries including sole proprietorships with no family involvement, pure family firms with only family management and family ownership, and joint ventures with other Taiwanese capitalists or even foreigners. I interviewed tanners who refuse to hire nonfamily managers and others who swear that only nonfamily members are suitable for the job. There is thus a wide diversity of organizational forms in the industry rather than one culturally preferred type. Most striking is the large number of tanners whose narratives reflect a strong professional identity.

Beyond the Firm: Corporate Networks

In the course of my research, several informants suggested that focusing on the family was an inadequate way of understanding the Taiwanese leather industry—and not only because Taiwanese capitalists manufacture goods in other organizational forms. Their main objection was that a focus on families and individual firms obscures relations among firms. Leather tanneries and related companies often invest in each other's companies, leading to a dense network of interrelated companies.[4] The Taiwanese word for corporate network is *koan-he khi-giap,* which means "network enterprise." Taiwanese people use this term in two ways. First, it can mean different companies owned by members of the same extended family. An example is the case of Li Ling-bing, the dentist turned tanner discussed above. The tannery, the food company, and the electronics company, run by three brothers, are considered to be network enterprises. Legally, however, they are all distinct enterprises, since each factory is registered in the name of the brother who actually runs it.

Second, the term network enterprise is also used to refer to cross-investment in firms owned primarily by nonfamily members. Li Ling-bing, for example, owns shares in Tai-hoa and Kiu-cheng, two prominent Tainan tanneries. Because of their co-investment relationships, Gak-heng, Tai-hoa, and Kiu-cheng are also considered to be network enterprises. The network enterprises of Senhoa Tannery include all of the individual tanneries that invested in that wettanning facility. Japanese anthropologist Ichiro Numazaki (1986) found that such networks span all Taiwanese industries, effectively linking highly capitalized Taiwanese firms to one another, as well as to government leaders and multinational corporations. In such networks, the fortunes of individual families have a minimal influence on the success or failure of individual firms, since other families have interests in the companies. Like other industries, the highly capitalized sector of leather tanning builds on greater networks, and the history of these networks reaches back into the Japanese colonial era.

In the leather industry, network enterprises develop on the basis of two kinds of relations: kinship and *tong-hang* (common occupation) relationships. The owners of Formosa Leather and Seng-li, for example, are paternal cousins. As I showed in my discussion of Formosa Leather's corporate history (Chapter 2), this tannery is one of Taiwan's oldest and was founded by a family that gained its wealth collaborating with the Japanese. The two tanneries are linked by kinship, and the younger owner of Seng-li gained experience at Formosa Leather before starting up his own tannery. Seng-li, the junior member, holds shares in Formosa Leather. Formosa Leather, the older tannery, however, does not own shares in Seng-li or, for that matter, in any other Taiwanese tannery. These two tanneries alone employ one out of ten workers in the industry's workforce and account for 13 percent of the capital invested in the industry.

Another kin-based network revolves around Kiu-cheng and Tai-hoa Tanneries (two of the major cowhide tanneries in Taiwan) and several smaller tanneries. Tai-hoa's president, Lo Chun-hiong, and Kiu-cheng's president, Loa Siu-heng, both worked at Formosa Leather but eventually left to set up their own tanneries. Tai-hoa was established in 1973 and quickly expanded to become one of Taiwan's largest modern tanneries. In addition to their tannery in Tainan, they also manufacture leather in Wenzhou, China, and have other investments in Thailand and New Zealand. Kiu-cheng started later, in 1986, and now produces leather at two tanneries in Taiwan, as well as in Thailand. These two companies are connected through affinal relations: Loa Siu-heng is Lo Chun-hiong's brother-in-law (his wife's younger brother). Their two tanneries lie across the street from each other in Tainan County. Due to their close kin relations, they refer to each other as network enterprises. Combined, they are also a formidable force in the leather industry, controlling 11 percent of the industry's registered capital and 13 percent of its workforce.

Their network enterprises also extend to other relatives who run smaller tanneries. Forty-one-year-old Ho Nai-ing, the *thau-ke-niu* ("boss lady"; see Chapter 5) at Hok-ling Tannery in Tainan County, provides one such example. Lo Chun-hiong of Tai-hoa is her maternal uncle, and Loa Siu-heng of Kiu-cheng is her aunt's elder brother. Her own career started out in commerce. After graduating from high school, she began work as a grain trader dealing in rice and beans. Then she worked at several companies as an accountant. To improve her business skills, she took courses in a variety of subjects, including computers and tax law. She started her career in leather with a job at Tai-hoa. Through such a wide variety of experiences, she said, she was able to learn how to operate a company on her own. Yet family connections in the corporate network were equally important.

She married Ong Tiong-ing, a leather trader who started out working in his cousin's tannery in Tainan. He later worked in sales at An-ping and then moved over to a management position at Formosa Leather. Eventually, however, he left to set up his own tannery with his personal savings, bank loans, and investment from both Tai-hoa and Kiu-cheng. They purchased land in 1978, built a factory and finally began production in 1987. Ho Nai-ing and her husband run the company together, and they have hired his younger brother to manage the tannery's wet tanning operations. So far, they have invested over NT$10 million dollars in their leather tannery. They also run a shoe factory in Taichung and have invested in a Chinese shoe factory.

Noting the complexity of their kin relations with other tanneries, I asked Ho Nai-ing why they don't pool their money and invest in one or two large factories. She replied that there are four main reasons why independent tanneries are better. First and most importantly, each individual factory has already invested a lot of capital in land and machinery, so none of them are prepared to shut down their own facilities to invest in another. Second, leather is a highly polluting industry, so it is better to spread it around the island rather than concentrating it all in one place. Thirdly, small size allows them to avoid intrusive government regulations. Finally, lower profits for each individual factory means that each factory is in a lower tax bracket. This allows them to pay lower taxes in total.

Even though kinship is clearly important in the evolution of these tanneries and the networks that bind them, Ho Nai-ing cautioned me against overemphasizing the family. In her small tannery of only thirty workers, two out of three of their management team are nonfamily members. A generation ago, she said, all factories preferred to hire family members, yet today only the few illegal underground factories still rely on kin. Most contemporary factories, however, now rely on outsiders for talent. In her words, "it's no longer fashionable to keep business in the family." Besides, she said, the technology all comes from outside Taiwan, as their chemical suppliers teach them how to tan leather, so there are few secrets in the industry. For a company to survive, she concluded, they have to open up and allow outsiders to take important management positions. Only then can they avoid the proverbial fate of family enterprises: wealth does not last beyond three generations. Since all of the tanneries in this group of firms employed professional managers, they did not consider themselves to be family enterprises.

In addition to corporate networks based on kinship, there are networks based on relations between former colleagues. Sin-chhi Tannery in Tainan County is one complex example of former colleagues cooperating together through co-investment. Ngo Tin-kui, the owner of the company, completed only six years of elementary school and started work at Formosa Leather at the age of fifteen. Now fifty-nine years old, he lived in Shenzhen, China, where he ran another tannery. His wife was not involved in tanning but worked as a professional manager in a textile factory. His twenty-eight-year-old son, however, had taken charge of the tannery in Taiwan.

In spite of this, he insisted that the tannery was not a family firm. When I asked if any relatives had invested in the company, I was told that cross-investment by relatives was rare. Since relatives rarely knew anything about leather, they were hesitant to risk their money in such an unknown venture. Ngo Tin-kui instead found three tanners who once worked as colleagues at An-ping and founded a tannery with their combined capital resources. They all invested in each other's companies. The owner of Tai-hoa, for example, invested in Sin-chhi, and the owner of Sin-chhi owned shares in Tai-hoa. Sin-chhi had three active and seven passive investors, none of whom were related by blood to Ngo Tin-kui. He explained: "In leather, it is rare for investors to be relatives. Instead tanners invest in each other's tanneries: I am your shareholder, you are my shareholder."

Ownership in Sin-chhi Tannery was very complex. Sin-chhi was actually three separate companies operating under the direction of one CEO, Ngo Tin-kui, and sharing a common secretarial staff of five women. I asked why they didn't just invest jointly in one large company. He said that this structure, divided into two separately owned dry-tanning facilities and one wet-tanning facility, helped prevent internal struggles among the three active investors in the company. The reason for these complex relations was economic. With the rising prices of land and tanning equipment, entry costs are too high for most individuals or families to open up a tannery on their own, as was once possible. With rising start-up costs, people need to set up joint partnerships with other people in order to accumulate enough capital to go into business. Former colleagues are likely candidates as partners.

Tong-hang relations influence not only co-investment patterns but also hiring and subcontracting relations. Professional managers sometimes follow their colleagues when one person leaves an existing tannery to set up a new company. In doing so, they can use their *tong-hang* affiliation, earned by working together, to gain a higher position and greater income in a new company. An example is forty-two-year-old Ngo Chhun-hui, who started her career at An-ping Tannery as an "office lady" taking care of administrative tasks. When her current boss left An-ping to set up a leather tannery, she went with him and was promoted to the post of production manager. Professional managers, as well as many tannery owners, concurred that knowledge of tanning is now far more important than kin relations to the owner in securing a job in management. Subcontracting also follows networks of former colleagues who once worked together in the same factory. Ngo Chhun-hui's company, for example, is a small tannery that does only part of the dry tanning process, tinting and spraying, for other companies. Their primary source of business is with former colleagues from An-ping, who now run their own tanneries.

Discussion

This and the preceding chapter show that identity in Taiwan, as manifested in entrepreneurial narratives, is multiple and fluid. Many of the characteristics labeled as "Chinese" or "Confucian," such as strong family structures, business orientation, diligence and thrift, and networking, are present in Taiwan and expressed clearly in these narratives. Yet, whether entrepreneurs label those institutions as Chinese or Taiwanese, a number of caveats must be made. Most importantly, these narratives show that familism is clearly not characteristic of all Taiwanese firms, as there is a wide diversity of firm organization in Taiwan.

Some tanners explicitly stressed that their firms were not family firms, since their wives and children had careers of their own. The fact that they felt a need to explain their family choices showed that they felt they were deviating from a cultural norm. Their life narratives, however, revealed the kind of professional identity with the impersonal and corporate form that one finds in the West. This can be attributed to the spread of business ideals in a time of globalization, or identification with a global ideoscape (Appadurai 1996: 33) of modernist management. These narratives thus run counter to the nationalist discourse that represents small firms in Taiwan as "Chinese family firms."

The discourse of the Chinese family firm carefully selects one kind of firm present in Taiwan and elevates it to a kind of national character. The critiques of this Orientalist discourse are numerous. Family firms dominate in many countries of the world, with Italy being one well-known example (Blim 1990). Networking is likewise not restricted to any particular culture but is common throughout the world, especially in circumstances of legal or political uncertainty, which make it difficult to rely on legal norms (Dirlik 1997: 314). The linking of Chinese-ness to one particular form of firm organization is thus related primarily to nationalist ideology.

In Taiwan, the nationalist discourse is especially problematic. Nationalist explanations of firm organization overlook the structural context that created those firms, including the influence of the Japanese colonial period and changes under Chinese Nationalist Party rule. By a discursive sleight-of-hand, native Taiwanese, marginalized by the Chinese Nationalist Party and forced to concentrate on unpleasant industries such as leather tanning, are labeled as the carriers of "Chinese" tradition because they do business within the family or networks of trusted kin and friends.

Arif Dirlik is correct in his argument that the discourse of Chinese capitalism ignores the wider structural context that creates small, flexible firms. In Taiwan, the discourse overlooks the process by which the Chinese Nationalist

Party took power in Taiwan and marginalized the native Taiwanese, thus leaving them to focus on small business. The business traits of relying on kinship and networks were so strong in their formative years precisely because the native Taiwanese distrusted the government brought in by the Mainlanders and preferred to do business within their own communities. As I witnessed repeatedly throughout my field research, those networks also become places for the remembering of Taiwanese identity, as entrepreneurs share stories of the past, tell jokes about Mainlanders, and discuss the identity politics of contemporary Taiwan. In spite of the traditional identity of "Chinese" family firms, the networks around these entrepreneurs have ironically strengthened non-Chinese forms of identity, whether as globe-trotting capitalists or as local citizens of Taiwan.

Arif Dirlik also argues that the discourse of Chinese capitalism suppresses the class, gender, and ethnic differentiations among the people encompassed within it (Dirlik 1997: 316). Within the leather tanning industry, moreover, there are important differences based on gender, class, and national belonging. All of these must be examined in order to untangle the webs of hegemony implicit in the sinicization of Taiwan. That is the goal of the next two chapters.

Notes

1. Replies add up to more than 100 percent due to multiple responses.

2. This translation of *xiaojie*, literally "little sister," is borrowed from the Japanese term for the position. Office ladies are not merely secretaries. In addition to answering the telephone, corresponding with other companies, and preparing tea, they often perform important financial and administrative tasks for their employers.

3. The same would also be true of a study of the Ford family, for example.

4. For more detailed discussion of Taiwanese corporate networks, see Greenhalgh (1984, 1988) and Numazaki (1986).

CHAPTER SIX

WOMEN AND ENTERPRISE

We Taiwanese didn't have a problem with the oppression of women. That is a problem that was brought in by outsiders, first by the Japanese and then by the Chinese. The older women in our families were aboriginals. They had a matriarchal society, and they had a lot of power. To this day, Native Taiwanese women have much more power in their families than Mainlander women.

—ARGUMENT MADE BY AN INTERLOCUTOR
AT A MARXIST STUDY GROUP, NATIONAL
CHENG KUNG UNIVERSITY, TAINAN, 1998

The Taiwanese are well known for their hospitality and they often approach foreigners to practice their English or just to chat. For anthropologists, these friendly gestures can provide new information and even important contacts. Once while relaxing in a Taipei park, for example, I noticed I was being watched by a young man wearing a stiff white shirt and carrying a briefcase. When I smiled at him, he walked over and offered me a cigarette. I declined, but he sat down and started to talk with me. He asked me where I was from; I said I was from America and came to Taiwan to do research on the leather tanning industry in southern Taiwan. His eyes lit up. "That's where I am from," he said. "I'm from Chiayi." He continued to explain that he was very familiar with the leather tanning industry, since he was a loan officer in a bank and served many of them as clients. His job, he said, was similar to mine in some ways since he needed to gather data on firms in order to evaluate their loan applications.

"I'll give you some advice," he said. "Whenever possible, interview the wives. The women usually know more about the business than the men, especially when it comes to financial matters. I myself prefer to deal with the women because they know more about what's going on in the companies than their husbands."

Although I insisted that I was more interested in Chinese culture than in company finances, I said I would remember his advice. I was initially surprised, since very little of the anthropological literature would have led me to anticipate his advice. The anthropological studies on family firms conducted in the heyday of Taiwan ethnography in the 1970s (de Glopper 1978; Niehoff 1987; Stites 1982, 1985) all focused on the family as a unit and paid scant attention to the different roles played by men and women in such businesses. Attention to women entrepreneurs, and the power held by women in family firms, came much later (for example, Gates 1996b; Simon 2003b).

BOSS-WIVES:
THE WOMAN BEHIND MANY A SUCCESSFUL MAN

I soon learned that the role of the wife in Taiwanese firms is so institutionalized that she even has a title in the local language. In Taiwanese firms, the male owner is referred to as the *thau-ke*, or boss. The word is composed of the characters for "head" and "family," to mean "boss." It suggests that a boss is head of the family, or head of the firm as a quasi-kinship group. In the many firms that are literally owned by families, the owner's wife is then referred to as the *thau-ke-niu*, or "boss-wife." The female term is complimentary rather than diminutive, often with an implication of participation and co-ownership in the enterprise. It is widely assumed in Taiwan that nearly every small company will have both a *thau-ke* and a *thau-ke-niu;* that is to say, both husband and wife will be involved in management. When women become *thau-ke*, they are often mistaken for *thau-ke-niu* or even employees (Simon 2003b: 208).

In the 1970s, Susan Greenhalgh found that the proportion of female family members working in Taiwanese firms decreased as business size increased (Greenhalgh 1994: 753). She argued, however, that women's roles were confined to the "inside" or domestic spheres, a division of labor that constricted women to their families of marriage: "*With few alternative sources of social identity,* women's fates were tied to their families of marriage, giving them few options but to play by those families' rules" (Greenhalgh 1994: 759, emphasis added). The subordination of women in these family firms was actively encouraged by the state in Mothers' Workshops during the Living Rooms as Factories campaign of the 1970s, when small-scale industrialization was taking off. In those classes, women were taught a reinterpretation of Confucian ethics that included a moral imperative to work in home factories for free (see Chapter 3).

Since industrialization and small factories were new to Taiwan, the use of Confucian ideology in a new context was clearly an "invention of tradition." In such images of national identity throughout the world, women are frequently represented as moral heroines. Jyoti Puri sees three types of linkages between women and nation: as reproducers of nations, as vessels of cultural nationalism, and as markers of boundaries between nations or ethnic groups (Puri 2004: 114). In the nationalistic construction imposed on Taiwan, images of women as obedient wives and virtuous mothers were used to represent the national identity of the Republic of China in a form of cultural nationalism.

This ideology, however, has not been unchallenged, as this chapter demonstrates. Taiwanese women contest the high moral claims of the Confucian discourse, for example, whenever they cite the proverb "Marry a chicken and follow a chicken; marry a dog and follow a dog." This proverb implies that patriarchal marriage norms are a less than noble tradition and actually a form of oppression. When women attribute this ridiculous-sounding proverb to Confucianism, they associate Confucianism and patriarchy with a feudal past incompatible with modernity.

Wanting to further explore Greenhalgh's hypotheses in my interviews, I asked the open-ended question, "What does the *thau-ke-niu* do in the tannery?" I soon discovered that the question itself was problematic, as it assumes that the owner's wife works in the tannery. That assumption proved to be wrong for nearly half of the firms studied. Some informants expressed impatience with the question, emphasizing to me that there is no *thau-ke-niu*, since the owner's wife has no connection at all to the tannery. It was thus not always possible to interview the wives, as I would have liked. Nonetheless, most interviewees provided information about the work of the boss's wife outside of their tanneries. Table 6:1 shows the role of the boss's wife in the tanneries I studied.

Table 6.1   Employment of Owners' Wives in Tanneries

Wife works in husband's tannery	37 (53%)
Housewife	15 (21%)
Wife has own career	9 (13%)
"No *thau-ke-niu*"	6 (9%)
Unmarried owner	1 (1%)
Tannery owned by woman	2 (3%)

Sources: Interviews with tannery owners, 1996–97.

Asking about wives, I found that slightly more than half of the owners' wives (thirty-seven out of seventy) work in their husbands' firms. Often men simply responded with "She helps out," in which case I pressed for more specific answers, wanting to learn if the women worked in management or in production. When they responded that she was a housewife, a sign of middle-class prestige, I inquired if she ever helped out in the tannery. By pressing further, I found that several "housewives" actually worked in the tanneries every day. Only in cases where I could determine without a doubt that the wife never worked in the factory did I classify her as a housewife. In cases where she worked in the tannery, I asked to interview her.

One typical example of a *thau-ke-niu* was fifty-three-year-old Ng Bi-hoa, whom I met in her Yunlin tannery. The shadows were growing in length when I arrived at their tannery at the end of the afternoon. I already had a handful of completed interview forms and pages of copious notes when I approached the final tannery for that day. At the end of the day, only two people were present in the tannery office: the *thau-ke* and his wife. Seeing that I was a foreigner, they graciously invited me to sit at the tea table and poured me the standard cup of oolong tea served to visitors. When I explained that I was interested in studying the Taiwanese leather tanning industry, the man said, "Why don't you stay for dinner? I have some work to do on the tannery floor. You can talk to my wife now, and then you can talk to me while we eat together."

Once her husband left the room, and as her daughter-in-law cooked at a stove in the back of the office, Ng Bi-hoa started telling me the story of her leather tannery. "Actually," she said, "this tannery was my idea. I did all of the work. If it weren't for my work, we would never have done this at all."

Continuing to tell me about the founding of her company, she said that she had worked until marriage as an accountant in a factory that made water faucets. While working there, she not only managed to accumulate savings but also learned important skills in business administration and management that would later be useful in her career.

After marriage, she left that job and her natal village to move to another village with her husband, the son of a policeman and a common worker in a leather tannery. She was not content with that life, however:

> I always wanted to go into business, but he [her husband] didn't. He thought it was enough to work in a factory. But I wanted to earn a lot of money, and I insisted that we go into business for ourselves. He already worked in a leather tannery, so I encouraged him to open his own tannery. It's better to be the owner than a worker, I said. Workers don't have enough money. So I thought of a way to open our own factory and we did it.

Using her own savings, money from her dowry, and a loan from a rotating credit association, she rented factory space in Taichung in 1971, and they

Figure 6.1   A powerful boss-wife and her husband.

started tanning on their own. She took charge of administration and management, while her husband took care of the technical aspects of tanning. By 1976, they had earned enough money to purchase land outside of her husband's village and build their own tannery with an initial investment of NT$180,000. As the tannery grew, they bought more automated machinery and slowly expanded production. Now, she boasted, there was no reason for either her or her husband to participate in the labor process at all, and they earned more than NT$100,000 a month. She still worked in management, managing finances, overseeing workers, and purchasing raw materials.

It was hard in the beginning. We had to work sixteen hours a day. We started work at 7:00 in the morning and couldn't rest until 11:00 at night. Often we had dinner at 1:00 in the morning. . . . Now we have a good income, and best of all we have leisure time. After going through so much hardship in my life, I like to travel a lot. I've been to Australia, the United States, Canada, Korea, and Japan.

Ng Bi-hoa asserted very strongly that the tannery had been built on *her* initiative, with *her* capital, and using *her* labor. Interviewing her, rather than relying on the assertions of her husband, thus showed that the supposedly "inside" roles of the *thau-ke-niu* do not necessarily imply subordination or lack of power. On the contrary, women can potentially gain significant power in family enterprises. The extent to which they do so depends on a complex web of factors, including the nature of specific industries, the position of manufacturing factories in the subcontracting system, and the personal ability of the women involved. Skilled women who build up trust and "strategic indispensability" during the establishment and development of a family firm can end up sharing equal power and responsibility with their husbands (Lu 1998). By doing so, they also construct professional identities that transcend mere attachment to their families of marriage.

WOMEN'S LABOR:
THE ROLE OF WIVES IN FAMILY TANNERIES

In most Taiwanese tanneries, there is a clear distinction between the space where manufacturing takes place and the space for living and eating.[1] In none of the seventy tanneries in my study did they combine manufacturing with living and eating space, although some tanneries did combine office and living space. In thirty of the tanneries studied, the families lived on the tannery premises, but in a building separate from the tanning facilities. In most tanneries, the owners commuted daily to the tannery, usually from the urban center nearest to the rural or suburban tannery.

One tanner in northern Tainan County, for example, commuted daily from Kaohsiung to go to work, a drive of over an hour. When I asked him why he preferred to live in Kaohsiung rather than near his tannery, he replied that the schools were better in Kaohsiung, and he wanted his children to get a good education. His concerns were thus not very different from middle-class families in North America who choose to live far from their workplaces so that their children can get a better education in suburban schools. With a higher standard of living, Taiwanese tannery owners have the luxury of not living in their tanneries, and thus avoiding the putrid smells and health hazards associated with the industry. When Taiwanese women work in their family tanneries, therefore, it is not merely an adjunct to the domestic duties performed in the house, but a career in itself.

The rate of women's participation in their husbands' firms remained steady across all size categories, with wives working in approximately half of the tanneries in each category. The largest tannery in which the wife worked employed 160 workers, but only six firms were larger than that. Like their husbands, *thau-ke-niu* working in larger tanneries tended to withdraw from the labor process and go into management as their firms expanded. Those who did not work in the labor process directly usually used management titles, such as "production manager" or "financial manager" to describe their jobs.

PUBLIC AND PRIVATE SPHERES

When asked about the division of labor by gender in their firms, men and women alike recited the common proverb, "Men are in charge of the outside and women are in charge of the inside." This means that men are in charge of "public" matters, and women are in charge of "private" matters. In only six of the thirty-seven firms where the wife worked in the tannery did the *thau-ke-niu* perform the public functions of public relations, sales, or raw hide purchasing. The most common reply was that women specialized in accounting and financial management, with fourteen of the thirty-seven women working in that capacity. Seven replied that the wife was in management, usually giving her the title of general manager. In those cases, she was in charge of both finances and labor management. Twenty-one out of thirty-seven wives, therefore, were in charge of the finances of their family businesses, exactly as my banker friend had predicted. In seven cases, the wife was the production manager, in charge of labor. In eleven cases, the wife worked in production, usually at the end of the production process, in trimming, measuring, and packaging. In nine cases, the wives were in charge of quality control and inventory. Most women managers performed more than one of the above tasks.

When talking about gender roles, some female informants used Mandarin Chinese terms to contrast women and men, describing women as having refined and meticulous hearts *(xixin)*, whereas men were described as having coarse and unrefined hearts *(cuxin)*. In reference to the human body, *xi* refers to slim builds, which are seen as ideal for women. *Cu* refers to strong, muscular builds, which are seen as ideal for men. Since women are seen as refined and meticulous, they are perceived as better at doing tasks that require attention to detail, including mathematics. Women frequently used this distinction between male coarseness and female attention to detail to explain to me why women often enter math-related professions such as banking, accounting, and stock trading. This distinction also applies to the jobs of women in family tanneries. As one woman told me:

> The *thau-ke-niu* is often in charge of quality control, since women are relatively strict and meticulous. Since women can notice every small detail, they are more careful. Men, on the other hand, are more coarse. My mother is quick to notice poor quality, as well as to notice what leather can be used

and for what purpose. Many tanneries, for example, just discard the left-over leather trimmings, but my mother knows how to collect them, fix them up, and then she sells them to mainland China.

The gendered division of labor between inside/private/female jobs and outside/public/male jobs should not be overdrawn, as the women who specialize in finances and accounting must deal with bankers and government officials. Furthermore, one cannot assume that "inside" jobs imply a lack of power. First, the wives who work in factories have power over their workers and are often expected to take over all of the tasks related to labor management. Second, those wives in charge of finances and accounting can actually exercise a good deal of control over their firms because they are in charge of the money. In those cases, men may do purchasing and sales, representing the firm to the outside world, but women are in charge of the daily operations of the tanneries. The women themselves often stressed the power they held and their crucial role in the tanneries, emphasizing a professional as well as family identity. As one woman said, "the *thau-ke-niu* is the busiest person in the factory."

Women who work hard in the public sphere receive a great deal of attention in the Taiwanese press. Successful career women, especially those in traditionally male fields, are referred to as *nuqiangren,* roughly translatable as "strong women." The attention given to *nuqiangren* has been criticized by feminist commentators, who point instead to the widespread economic subordination of women in Taiwanese society. The term also has subtle negative connotations, as it implies that the woman is not skilled at the traditional virtues of taking care of men and children. I encountered many capable, strong women in contexts ranging from the factory floor to brokerage firms. None of them used the term *nuqiangren* to describe themselves. Even when asked by myself or others if they perceived themselves in such terms, they replied that their hard work did not qualify them as *nuqiangren.*

ASSERTING FEMALE AGENCY

Life histories of the *thau-ke-niu* in Taiwan's tanneries illustrate that the nation's tanneries were often built with women's skills, knowledge, and capital. Women commonly described their family firms as partnerships between husband and wife. It was common, in fact, for the husband to supply technical expertise and the wife to provide business experience and financial acumen.

An example was Iam-sui Tannery run by Lim Ken-seng and his wife Kho Le-koat in Tainan County. Their small pigskin tannery had provided them a comfortable lifestyle, including two Mercedes-Benz automobiles and a large home. They lived on the factory premises, separate from the tanning facilities, but in the same building as the office. Outside the building was a small traditional garden—a pond, a large stone symbolizing a mountain, and an artificial waterfall. The interior was tastefully decorated with Chinese antiques.

Mr. Lim was born in 1953 to a family of fish farmers in rural Tainan County. He had four elder brothers, one younger brother, and three older sisters, all of whom still raised fish for a living. After graduating from high school and completing military service, he went to work in a leather tannery in Kaohsiung, planning to open up a factory of his own when he learned enough about tanning.

His elder brother introduced him to Kho Le-koat while he was still working in Kaohsiung. Her family, in Lukang, ran a food-processing factory, so she learned some business skills from her parents. After graduating from high school, she went to work in the merchandising section of a Christian hospital in Changhua. "That was business," she insisted. "The hospital even sent me back to school to study accounting and business administration."

In 1978, they got married. That same year they opened up a tannery with capital given to them by Mr. Lim's father. I asked them how they divided up their tasks in the tannery. In a family tannery, explained Mr. Lim, they didn't use formal titles, and they weren't very systematic about job assignments. They shared management duties, and both of them did sales. He was in charge of the technical aspects, and sometimes worked in the labor process when they were short of workers. She answered the phone, took care of the company's finances, supervised incoming raw materials, shipped the finished leather, and managed labor.

An even more obvious example of women's power in the industry was the Tiong-ing Tannery of Pingtung County. I interviewed the owner's daughter, a recent graduate from a Canadian university, in the reception area on the second floor of the tannery. The office was plushly decorated, with leather furniture, wood walls, and a large window overlooking the tannery operations. A stereo was set up next to the sofa, along with a large collection of American CDs and an illuminated crystal statue of Guanyin, the Buddhist goddess of mercy.

She told me the history of how her parents set up a joint venture in Pingtung. Her father was from Taichung, and her mother from Pingtung. They both studied chemistry in college and met while working in the sales division of a Taichung chemical company. After they got married, they decided to start their own company, preferring to work for themselves. One of her mother's friends in Pingtung was interested in buying a leather tannery and asked them to invest in a partnership. In 1973, the couple moved back to her mother's home in Pingtung and entered into a joint venture with that friend. As for their portion of the joint venture, half of the start-up capital came from her mother's father. The other half was a combination of their savings from work and her dowry. At first, they knew nothing about leather and had to rely on their business partner to learn the technical aspects of the business.

Three years after the firm was established, they discovered that the partner was embezzling profits from the leather he sold. Unable to resolve their financial disagreements about how to remit profits, they divided the company into two tanneries, with the two families working side by side in one factory complex. Eventually, the other tannery sold out to them, moving their production to China.

Since the family lived in Pingtung with the wife's family, and her father contributed half of the capital, the organization of labor in the firm was based on the wife's natal family. The wife's father was listed as the president of the company, although he did not participate in the daily operation of the tannery. The husband was the general manager. The wife was in charge of quality control and inventory. The wife's younger brother was the production manager. Their daughter worked in sales. Two other children, one son and one daughter, were attending school in Vancouver but planned to return to Taiwan upon graduation to work in their family's tannery.

These three case histories demonstrate the wide range of possibilities for wives in family factories. In the first case, a man and woman opened up a tannery together, but the woman perceived it as the product of her own ambition, capital, and talent. In the second case, the man provided technical skills and the woman provided business experience and acumen. They described themselves as equal partners. In the third case, the family firm was a joint venture between the husband and the wife's father. This tannery followed a matrilocal pattern simply because a business opportunity arose in the wife's hometown. This was a significant change from traditional rural society, which is both patrilocal and patrilineal. In agricultural communities, women were expected to live with their husband's families, and they often had little contact with their natal families after marriage. Industrialization in Taiwan has changed these expectations, since many women maintain close emotional and financial ties with their natal families after marriage. In all of these cases, the women were able to assert professional identities instead of merely identifying with their families of marriage.

The life histories of boss-wives reveal that women are not necessarily subordinate to their husbands in family firms. Their contributions are crucial, as they provide labor, skills, capital, and business contacts. Their role, in fact, is more complementary than subordinate, as the women are likely to point out in their own personal narratives. These women invested capital, skills, and hard labor in their family businesses and reaped the rewards of a higher standard of living. Through these work narratives they assert independent professional identities.

WOMEN'S LABOR: DAUGHTERS AND DAUGHTERS-IN-LAW

When Taiwan was still predominantly an agricultural society, daughters were expected to work on their parents' farms until marriage; after marriage they would leave the farm and work for their husbands. Daughters-in-law married into their husbands' families and worked for their husbands' parents. Many contemporary tanners, however, claim that young people no longer wish to work in tanneries, and owners must revise their business plans accordingly. At the Iam-sui Tannery, for example, I asked if the owner's children, an eighteen-year-old daughter and a sixteen-year-old son, ever helped out in the factory.

Mr. Lim said, "Children no longer work in Taiwanese family factories because they have to use their time to study. Twenty years ago, they worked in the factories, but now they study a lot and try to go as far as they can in school, the further the better."

I asked, "Do they plan to work in the tannery in the future, perhaps in management?"

Mr. Lim replied, "No. They'll study whatever they're interested in. Nowadays, most young people don't stay in their family's business. They all want to pursue careers of their own."

"What are your children interested in?" I asked.

"Nothing but play!" interrupted *thau-ke-niu* Kho Le-hoat with a hearty laugh.

A "Traditional" Family

The few tanneries that still rely on family labor are rare, and they proudly boast that they are more traditional than their competitors. One example was Mr. Chiong's tannery in rural Kaohsiung County. One of the older tanneries in my study, this firm still maintained the tradition of employing kin for all of the important management and technical positions. The elder Mr. Chiong started tanning during the Japanese occupation, working in a Japanese-run tannery in Tainan. After the Japanese left Taiwan, he set up his own factory with his wife and slowly expanded it using the labor and skills of his sons and daughters-in-law.

Their eldest child was a girl. She worked in the tannery until she married, at which time she left to live with her husband in a nearby town. Their second child was also a girl. She, too, married and left, but unfortunately her husband died, leaving her alone with two sons. She had returned to her parents' home and now worked in the trimming section of the tannery. Her two sons, now grown, worked as technicians in the factory. The return of a daughter to her parents' home and the incorporation of her children into her natal family illustrate clearly the flexibility of Taiwanese families. Nonetheless, the contributions of daughters are often less valued than those of sons, as demonstrated by the career histories of her younger brothers.

The third child, the eldest son, was now the president of the tannery. He was married, and his sons worked in the lower ranks of management in the firm. His wife worked in the trimming section. The fourth child, a son, worked as a chemical technician in the tannery, and his wife worked in trimming and finishing. He had one son, a technician in the tannery, and three daughters, none of whom worked in tanning. Nonetheless, they did help out in their own ways, said their father with pride. His second daughter worked in a bank and was in charge of foreign exchange. She helped the tannery conduct the foreign currency transactions needed in such a global industry.

The fifth child was also a son. He worked in the tannery, sorting the finished leather by quality. His wife worked in trimming and finishing. He had two daughters and two sons, including one son old enough to work in the tannery as a technician. The sixth child, a son, was the only one of his generation to attend school beyond primary school. He studied shipbuilding at National Taiwan Ocean University in Keelung and was now in management in a shipbuilding company. Their seventh and last child was a daughter, who married out and now lived with her husband in a nearby town. Their family history clearly reflected the gender expectations they held for their children. Daughters married out and worked with their husbands, no longer considered part of the family. The only daughter who worked in the family was a widow who returned to her natal family after her husband's death.

A New Generation of Women: Opting Out or Giving In

In the second generation, men are much more likely to work in their father's companies than are daughters or daughters-in-law. Of the fifty-eight firms from which I was able to get detailed hiring information, forty-three (74 percent) hired relatives in management, primarily sons. Daughters and daughters-in-law are less likely to work in family tanneries. I found only six firms (10 percent) with unmarried daughters, seven firms with married daughters (12 percent), and fourteen firms (24 percent) with daughters-in-law on staff. Usually, these young women were employed as accountants. In those fifty-eight firms, I found forty-five sons working for their fathers, compared to fifteen daughters working for their fathers and eighteen women working for their fathers-in-law.

It is a rational strategy for men to work in their fathers' firms, as they are well positioned to eventually take over the firm. Daughters, on the other hand, play a more marginal role in the firms and are unlikely to ever take control of the tanneries, especially if they have to compete with brothers for key positions. Daughters-in-law can aspire to take the more powerful position of *thau-ke-niu* when the father retires and hands over control to the son. Even then, however, tanning is seen as a sunset industry in Taiwan, and most young women are aware that their tanneries might not last long enough to give them positions of power and wealth. It is not surprising, therefore, that many young women choose not to work for family tanneries and elect to find jobs elsewhere instead. This is also an expression of contemporary women's professional identities.

The younger generation of women, much better educated than their parents, takes a cynical view of traditional gender expectations. One twenty-eight-year-old unmarried woman, a graduate of the University of California, worked at her father's tannery in rural Kaohsiung County. Because of her English skills, she did most of the import and export transactions for the tannery. She also worked in packaging, dealt with the bank, sold the baseball gloves they produced, and even stood on the production line if needed to fill in for an absent worker. Her mother was the company's financial officer, in charge of all of the company's financial decisions. I remarked that she and her mother were both *nuqiangren* and made important contributions to their family tanneries. "In Taiwan," she said cynically, "there is no such thing as a strong woman. Even if they work hard, their contributions are unrecognized."

As I took down her family history, she explained to me the gender expectations that women face as they grow up. "Once daughters marry out," she said, "they don't work for their parents anymore. They work for their own families." Her attitude toward these expectations was cynical—especially since she had studied feminism in California—yet resigned, because her parents viewed that as foreign ideology. I asked if she planned to work in her father's tannery after marriage. She said it all depended on her husband's job. If he owned a company, she would work for him. If he didn't have his own company, she would choose her job depending on where they lived, working in the tannery only if they lived nearby and her husband gave her permission to work there. "It all depends on my own family," she said. "If there are disagreements, I will side with my husband."

She knew for sure, however, that she preferred more than anything to have her own career. In the past, she said, men preferred for their wives to stay at home, but now many women pursued their own careers. She said that it was better for women to work outside the family. Otherwise, they spent all of their time at home and were unaware of what happened in the outside world. "Their husbands have affairs, and they don't even know about it," she said. "I have no faith in family. I don't believe in men at all." Having explored feminist thought in the United States, she was conscious of the structural limitations of patriarchy. For some women, the best way to assert autonomy in such a context is through owning their own business. Two tanneries in Taiwan, in fact, are owned by women.

A FEMALE TANNER: THE FAMILY LEGACY CONTINUES

Amidst the rice fields of Tainan County sits an unimposing small tannery run by four sisters and their mother. On a cool February afternoon, I arrived at the tannery on motorcycle with a friend from Tainan. There was no gate-keeper, so I cautiously entered the factory and asked the first worker I saw if the *thau-ke-niu* was in. He indicated that we should talk with Ms. Chiu, a young mannish woman with glasses and closely cropped hair. I told her that I was doing a historical study of Taiwanese family tanneries and would like to interview the *thau-ke-niu*. "There is no *thau-ke-niu* here," she said matter-of-factly, "but you can interview me. My father started the tannery."

She escorted me into her spartan office for the interview, where she served us root beer and hard candy left over from the Chinese New Year, which had been celebrated the week prior to our interview. As I took down her family genealogy, I discovered that she herself was the *thau-ke*. The tannery, now in its second generation, had passed into her hands because her father died without a male heir.

Her family had a long history of tanning and proved to have one of the more complex genealogies I studied, as nearly everyone in her extended family was engaged in leather tanning. Her grandfather began tanning during the Japanese period and continued to work as a leather splitter at a large tannery in Tainan City after the Japanese left in 1945. He died in 1953. His two sons, splitters in the same tannery, both left that tannery in the 1970s to establish their own tanneries with their wives. His daughter married an apprentice splitter from the elder brother's tannery, and they set up a tannery together.

The eldest son died in 1994, passing the tannery to his wife and four un-married daughters. The eldest daughter had completed high school, as well as three years of training at a prestigious management school in Taipei. Now thirty-four years old, she had taken over the position of president. She said she was capable of running a tannery not only because of her formal educa-tion but also because she had been observing her father run the company ever since she was a small child. Nonetheless, she was modest about her achievements. She said, "I had to take over from my father. But I just do the work that I have to do, and then after work my time is my own."

When I remarked that I had met very few female bosses, she replied,

> That's because there are so few. A lot of women own their own companies, but very few run factories. It's difficult for a woman to do business, because business is often a male affair, and men like to drink when they talk busi-ness. It's hard for women to enter into such circles, since it's hard for them to get along with men. But I still do well, because I produce high quality goods, and I can rely on my father's old customer base.

Noting her age, I asked if she planned to marry in the near future. Ms. Chiu replied, "If I find a partner, I'll get married. If I don't find a partner, I just won't get married. But if I get married, I'll have even more problems in my life than I do now." Curious, I asked, "Do you mean because you will have to take care of children as well as run a factory?" She said, "It is worse than that. I would have to deal with his family! They would meddle with the tannery affairs."

Ms. Chiu's history illustrates two important things about the Taiwanese economy. First, it demonstrates that property inheritance is flexible and can go down the female line if no male heirs are available. Second, it suggests that despite this flexibility such ownership is not always recognized by all of the members of the community. Ms. Chiu's own fears that any prospective in-laws would interfere in business reveal the problems that women face when they inherit property and want to maintain full control of it. She will probably choose lifetime celibacy in order to keep her tannery and her own professional autonomy safe from the ambitions of outsiders.

A Female Tanner: Hard Work and Capital

Another female tanner, however, had no such fears. Hard work and capital have secured her place in the industry. Greenhalgh (1994: 756) argues that acquired property bears more prestige and power than inherited property. Acquired property is viewed as belonging to the person who earned it, whereas inherited property is seen as belonging to the male lineage. This difference may explain the different perceptions of these two women toward their industrial property, as well as their prospects for asserting a strong professional identity.

Ms. Chhoa of Yunlin County was the only woman I encountered who built up a tannery exclusively with her own capital and talents. An extraordinarily busy woman of nearly sixty, she refused to be interviewed for my study but permitted me to interview her daughter-in-law, an accountant in the company, while she herself conducted business negotiations with clients in the same room.

Ms. Chhoa was born in rural Changhua County in 1938. She completed only a primary school education and married at the age of twenty. She started out in business by renting a storefront and opening up a music store. In the 1980s, she started investing in industrial land and made a lot of money from the boom in land prices during that period. She closed down her music store and, using her profits from land speculation, bought into a glove factory with a male partner. She started recycling the scraps of leather from the glove factory and then decided to specialize in the recuperation of leather scraps. With the right equipment and finishing, she found that she could shred leather scraps and mold them into sheets of recycled leather, which look like regular leather on the surface and can be used in such products as furniture upholstery. Her partner sold out his share in the company, went into leather trading, and eventually raised the money to set up his own tannery.

Like many Taiwanese companies, Ms. Chhoa's tannery listed seven stockholders, which allowed them to register as a limited partnership. That legal status has certain tax advantages and limits their personal liability in the event of bankruptcy. They listed the owners as Ms. Chhoa, her two sisters, a daughter-in-law, her husband, a brother-in-law, and a nephew—in that order. Each stockholder was in charge of a different aspect of the business, she said, which reduced conflicts. Ms. Chhoa's husband played no role in management, as his job was merely to maintain the firm's technical equipment. I asked why Ms. Chhoa was the president of the company rather than her husband.

"Of course she's the president," she replied impatiently. "She started the factory with her own capital, so the company belongs to her!"

The strong role played by women in tanneries is not necessarily a recent phenomenon. The owners of one tannery in Chiayi attributed the origin of their tannery exclusively to the work of their mother, Tan Chui-hoa. When I questioned them about the history of their factory, they proudly showed me pictures of their mother and a copy of her identity card. She was born in Chiayi in 1934. Her father was one of the first tanners in the area, having entered the craft during the Japanese occupation of Taiwan, and she learned tanning from her father.

In the 1950s, she married a military policeman from Shandong Province, who had come to Taiwan in 1949 with the Kuomintang. Using her own skills and capital, she opened up her own tannery in 1958. Her three sons still recognized her crucial role in the tannery and referred to the firm not as a family factory but rather as a company started by their mother. Strong women such as Tan Chui-hoa may have been rare, but their stories demonstrate that industrialization in Taiwan has offered opportunities to skilled and intelligent women from the very beginning. In fact, ethnographies of Taiwan in the 1960s show that rural women had long held "private money" that could be invested in such things as grain associations, livestock, land, and even shops. All investment proceeds remained in their control rather than that of their families (Cohen 1976: 178–184). Since the precedents for independent women's economic behavior already existed at the beginning of industrialization, it is no surprise that some women have contested patriarchal discourses of "Confucianism" and asserted strong, new identities for themselves.

DISCUSSION

In my study of family-run tanneries, I found that women play crucial roles in their family firms. Like Gates (1996b), I found that capitalist enterprises give women wealth, social power, and prestige. As *thau-ke-niu*, they make important contributions in labor, skills, business acumen, and even capital. They assert their own power and contributions in their personal life narratives, often taking credit entirely for the success of their firms. Their contributions are recognized by both male and female relatives as they age, and they reap the rewards of their labor through a better standard of living. Their roles can be seen not as subordinate but as complementary to those of men. This complementary relationship generally assigns the "outside" business roles to men and the "inside" roles to women. Both men and women, however, assert professional identities in their personal narratives.

When their marriages are successful, women perceive their work in family firms as rational and profitable individual strategies. One woman in her early thirties, for example, perceived her career as a *thau-ke-niu* as far more rational than my choice to pursue a Ph.D. in anthropology. She explained her perspective:

> I don't understand why you want to get a Ph.D. Look at me. I'm the same age as you. I only graduated from high school, but I have a factory, a nice house, a family, and a BMW. You go to school, and you learn a lot, but you don't have any of those things. Some people think it's worth going to school for so long after you graduate. But will you be earning more money than me five years from now? I don't think so.

Despite the lingering Chinese Nationalist ideology that stresses obedience to men, the lives of Taiwanese women have changed from the days when, as peasant women, they went from working on their fathers' farms to working on their husbands' farms. Margery Wolf once remarked that "a truly successful Taiwanese woman is a rugged individualist who has learned to depend largely on herself while appearing to lean on her father, her husband, and her son" (Wolf 1972: 41). As strong women become more visible in Taiwan, and now that a woman is vice president of the country, there is less need for women to keep up the appearance of subordination.

The expansion of the economy under a capitalist regime has increased opportunities for women to succeed as individuals both inside and outside of the family context. As *thau-ke-niu,* they can gain power in an industrial setting. Alternatively, they can run businesses of their own, even in a seemingly masculine industry like leather tanning. Attention to women's voices reveals that women play a stronger role in Taiwanese families and family firms than an androcentric "Confucian" ideology would allow.

The contradiction between women's narratives and the discourse of Confucianism is important in Taiwan because of the connections between the latter and Chinese nationalist ideology. The emphasis on Taiwanese women as the bearers of Chinese tradition in this nationalist story is superficially reminiscent of Indian nationalist stories that are similarly based on dichotomies of inner/outer, home/world, and feminine/masculine. As in Chinese nationalist narratives told in Taiwan, women in Indian nationalism stood for the spiritual qualities of the nation through "traditional" qualities of self-sacrifice, benevolence, devotion, and so forth (Chatterjee 1993: 131). The difference between the two nationalist narratives, of course, is that Indian nationalism was a reaction to British colonialism whereas Chinese nationalism in Taiwan was introduced by outsiders in order to justify their rule over Taiwan. It is for this reason that Confucianism had to be reconstructed and taught to women by the state through educational campaigns. It is also for this reason that women contest the narratives and assert their own positions of power. By doing so, they mark Confucianism as a remnant of the past and identify themselves as something other than Chinese.

Note

1. For comparison with the conditions of Hakka Chinese tanners in Calcutta, where tanners actually live in the tanneries, see Oxfeld (1993).

CHAPTER SEVEN

WORKERS AND BOSSES

M r. Kho, owner of a small Tainan County tannery, laughed heartily when I told him I was doing a study of the Taiwanese leather industry. "You'll never learn anything from books," he said. "The only way you can understand tanning is to do it yourself." Furthermore, he would be receiving a large shipment of hides in a few days and was "short on labor." He would be happy to hire me as a temporary unpaid worker for two days. The arrangement would benefit us both, he said in jest, as he would get extra help for free, and I would get an education. Anxious to experience tannery work myself, I immediately accepted his generous offer.

Mr. Kho called me as soon as the hides, imported from the United States, cleared customs in Kaohsiung and were delivered to his tannery. He warned me to wear old clothes that I would not mind destroying, since the work would be dirty and hard. I nervously arrived the next morning wearing my oldest shirt and a pair of deteriorating blue jeans. Mr. Tan, a technician, took me into the factory. The tanning drums were already up and running, making a loud rumbling noise and emptying leather, along with streams of bluish water, onto the floor. Several men wearing high boots waded into the water to pick up the tanned hides cast from the drums and threw them into piles nearby. I sighed with relief as we passed that section full of smelly polluted water and went into the next. Mr. Tan started me on my first job, working with two older men on a press that removes excess moisture from leather. The machine is imported from Italy, he explained with evident pride.

I worked alongside a gray-haired man in a white tank top, who patiently explained how to place the sheets of leather on the flat surface, and then flatten them out with a hand tool resembling the squeegees used to wash cars. As soon as six sheets of leather had been placed on the press and covered all available space, the machine operator pushed the button on the control panel and the top of the press came down. It revealed a second layer where six sheets of pressed leather waited to be removed and replaced with six unpressed sheets. The dual levels allowed us to place one set of leather on the machine and smooth out the wrinkles, while the machine pressed out the second layer. The machine has a temperature of 100 degrees Celsius, explained my co-worker, so I should be careful not to touch the metal surface directly with my hands. Nonetheless, he emphasized, the machine has a built-in safety device that makes it impossible for us to accidentally press our hands. To demonstrate, he lightly touched the orange-colored guard rail that wraps around the press. The machine came to an immediate halt.

It took me about half an hour to learn how to identify which side of the leather should be face up (the side with minor traces of hair) and to learn how to smooth out the wrinkles efficiently. According to Mr. Tan, they can add 2 to 3 percent to the surface area of the leather by smoothing it out as flat as possible, thus increasing the price of the finished product. The men worked slowly, smoking as they worked and taking occasional breaks whenever we finished one batch and had to wait for more leather to be brought to our machine.

Suddenly at noon, a whistle sounded. The rumble of the tanning drums came to a slow halt. The machine operator stopped the leather press machine. We put our now-wet gloves on the press to dry and left to eat. Mr. Tan, the technician, invited me to eat in the office with him. Technicians, managers, and workers all ate the same packaged lunches and soup provided by the factory. The managers ate at a table in the office, while the workers ate outside or in the factory, wherever they found a relatively clean place on the ground to sit.

After lunch everyone took an afternoon nap. The office ladies slept at their desks. In the factory, workers stretched out on the floor near their machines, using sheets of leather as blankets to keep off the cold. The place was completely silent, except for the sound of the birds outside in the rice fields. At one o'clock, a whistle sounded again. Everyone slowly arose, wiping the sleep from his or her eyes. The tanning drums started to rotate and everyone returned to work.

In the afternoon, I went back into the factory. This time Mr. Tan put me on a splitting machine that splits leather into two layers: stiff upper leather and softer split leather. There were five people on this machine. One middle-aged woman lifted the hides off a platform and gave them to the two men who op-

Figure 7.1   Tannery work: splitting hides.

erated the splitting machine. They pushed the hides through the splitting machine, which cut each one into two layers. The older of the two men, a master technician, kept an eye on the thickness of the leather, measuring it occasionally and adjusting the machine as we changed batches.

I stood on the opposite side of the machine from Ms. Tiu, a hefty woman in her forties. Our job was to remove the two layers of leather from the machine and place them in piles on carts behind us. She was in charge of the upper layer, folding the leather as it came out of the machine, and placing it on the cart. I took care of the split leather. In the first batch, the upper leather was so thick that the remaining lower leather was thin and disintegrated in my hands as I pulled it from the machine. My job was to put it on a cart so it could be taken away and discarded. For the latter two batches, however, both the upper and split leathers were thick enough to be used. I had to fold the split leather and put it on the cart.

After working for about half an hour, Ms. Tiu asked me if I found the hides, about fifteen kilograms a piece, to be too heavy. No problem, I replied. I work out in the gym every day and am accustomed to lifting heavy weights. In fact, by working in the factory I was missing a good workout in which I would bench-press up to sixty kilograms. But as time passed, my muscles got sorer and sorer. I soon realized I wasn't missing my workout after all, just getting a different one than usual! My body soon adjusted to the rhythm of the work, hide after hide being pulled through the splitting machine. And with a talkative co-worker at my side, I didn't even notice the passage of time.

Looking at the western brands on the skins, I tried to imagine them as cows and wondered what the American family was like who raised those cattle in Texas or Oklahoma. I remarked to Ms. Tiu that I found it interesting—not long ago, this hide was a cow. Then they separated it into meat and hides. The meat became steaks for Americans to eat, and the hides came here to be made into shoes. She let out a hearty laugh and asked me questions about America. "Do a lot of people raise cows?" I said yes, the population density is lower than Taiwan, so there is plenty of room to raise cows, and the climate is more appropriate for raising cattle there than in subtropical Taiwan. "Do Americans eat steak every day?" she asked. I said, "No, it would be boring to eat the same thing every day." She laughed and continued to work.

At the end of the day, Ms. Tiu asked if my arms were sore. I said yes, and asked if hers were. She said no, she's used to it. I asked if they got sore when she first started working there. She said yes. I remarked that it was a very difficult and strenuous job. Not at all, she insisted. It's just a matter of getting accustomed to the labor.

The following day, I returned to the tannery. This time, Mr. Tan took me to the wet tanning area and said I would be working there, dragging the wet skins from the tanning drums. I looked at the workers, three shirtless Thai men, soaking wet and wallowing through bluish water in high rubber boots. Disgusted by the prospect of becoming soaking wet with highly polluted water, I wavered and asked if I could do a less dirty job. Mr. Tan laughed at me, declaring, "Only those who have worked in the water can say they've made leather!" Yet he agreed that I could work elsewhere, helping out the *obaasan,* a term for older women, derived from the Japanese word for grandmother.

He assigned me a job tinting leather with a woman in her fifties. Our job was to place finished leather on a conveyor belt, making sure it was flat and right side up. The leather then went into the machine, where an automatic sprayer tinted it. When we finished each batch, one of the male technicians came over and set up the machine with a new color. Each time they had to test one or two pieces to make sure it came out the right color. Since the woman had been doing this job for six years, she was quite skilled. Occasionally, she left me alone at the machine, stepping over to the control panel to make adjustments and help the technician with the machinery.

I spent the entire day working with her, except for about half an hour at the end of the day when the owner, Mr. Kho, called me outside to work at another machine in the sunny courtyard. He and I worked together on a machine used to wet down dry hides. I fed the large, dry cowhides into the machine, and he pulled them out at the other end. I said I was amazed to see how management jumped right into the labor process. He attributed that behavior to the scale of his factory, saying that it was often necessary for owners to do manual labor in small tanneries because they have a shortage of workers.

AN ANTHROPOLOGY OF LABOR

No ethnography of manufacturing would be complete without attention to workers. By any standards, workers, as a group, make up one of the largest segments of the Taiwanese population. The percentage of the labor force in manufacturing rose from a mere 16.9 percent in 1952 and 20.5 percent in 1960 to 42.4 percent in 1980, but decreased to 40 percent by 1990 and to less than 35 percent by the end of 2003 (Wang 1993: 196; Executive Yuan Council of Labor Affairs 1995: 34–35; Executive Yuan Council of Labor Affairs 2003: 20). In 1994, the percentages of the employed labor force working in agriculture, manufacturing, and services was 11 percent, 39 percent, and 50 percent, respectively, showing only a slight decrease in manufacturing at the time this research was conducted (Executive Yuan Council of Labor Affairs 1995: 34–35).

Of course the number of workers far exceeds that of factory owners. My study of the southern Taiwanese tanning industry covers a manufacturing process that touches the lives of 4,300 tannery workers but only 72 tannery owners. There are thus sixty times as many workers as owners in the industry. As tannery workers have a different relation to the mode of production than the bosses, they constitute a class. Yet the objective existence of a group of workers with interests different from that of factory owners is only part of the story. Contrary to orthodox Marxist assumptions that capitalism should lead to antagonism between capitalists and workers, Taiwan has managed to avoid confrontational labor relations and the rise of a powerful autonomous labor union movement. How has Taiwan managed to avoid contentious labor relations? How is this related to complex relations between identities based on class, ethnicity, and nation?

Classical Marxist approaches to labor relations assumed a polar opposition between workers and capitalists, with capitalists exploiting the surplus value created by the laboring masses. One of the central problems in Marxist anthropology is when and under what circumstances workers will unite as a class opposed to capitalist exploitation. Marx made a distinction between "class-in-itself" and "class-for-itself," the difference being the presence or absence of class consciousness. Class-in-itself refers to an objective social group defined by the relationship of its members to the means of production, regardless of whether individuals perceive themselves as members of a united class. Once workers construct a group identity as a unified class with interests opposed to another distinct capitalist class, they constitute a class-for-itself. At this point, Marx assumed that class struggle would develop, along with the demand for direct worker control of the means of production (Marx 1982).

Attempts to put class analysis in a cultural and historical framework began with Marx. In *The Eighteenth Brumaire,* he described a situation where small-holding peasants in France lacked self-identity or common organization as a class because the French state took a series of measures to cajole and appease smallholders (Marx 1963). In a similar vein, social historian E. P. Thompson (1965) examined the specific historical conditions by which working-class consciousness arose in England, focusing on such historical and ideological factors as the Protestant history of dissent, the working-class mob culture of rebellion that developed out of a common history of oppression, and an official state ideology of equal rights which stood in sharp contrast to the daily reality of oppression and poverty experienced by most workers. As a product of history, he argued, class is not a "thing" but rather a "happening" (Thompson 1978: 295). It is thus a very important form of identity, although it may conflict with other identities and thus lose effectiveness.

Anthropologists have often done well at analyzing class consciousness in specific contexts. Issa Shivji (1976), for example, showed that class formation in Tanzania is based on two factors: position in the relations of production and ethnic identity. Classes are not merely abstract categories, he argued, but groupings of people who act collectively. Forms of identity not based on production relations, such as ethnic identity, may take precedence and prevent the formation of unified class consciousness. These kinds of Marxist approaches remain relevant to a study of Taiwanese labor relations.

In this chapter, I look first at evidence of class identity in contemporary Taiwan. I then examine the role of the state in labor relations, arguing that peaceful labor relations have been primarily a result of the carrot-and-stick policies of the Chinese Nationalist Party on Taiwan. I then turn my attention to labor relations at the factory level, the various ways in which Taiwanese industrialists "manufacture consent" (Burawoy 1979, 1985) in their companies. I begin with one of the most striking instances of class identity I observed among Taiwanese workers, the workers' demonstration on International Labor Day.

MAY DAY IN TAIPEI, 1997

On May 1, 1997, I went to Taipei to participate in a demonstration of workers from all over Taiwan. The demonstrators, gathered at the Taipei train station, were clearly visible from far away due to the large yellow flags carried by members of the Telecommunications Union and the Petroleum Workers' Union. The square outside the station was even more bustling than usual. Amidst train passengers streaming out of the station and street peddlers hawking their goods, labor organizers distributed pamphlets to passersby and organized the arriving workers for the planned demonstration. Each participant was asked to sign in upon arrival so that organizers could estimate the numbers present at the demonstration. Organizers from several unions distributed black prison shirts to all of the demonstrators, asking them to wear them as a visual symbol protesting the weak position of labor in Taiwan. Migrant workers were notable only in their absence.

After about one thousand people had gathered at the Taipei train station, the demonstration began. One by one, different groups of workers, each organized by a different union, marched out of the train station in a silent and orderly formation. The stars of the event, a group of eighty-five female garment workers on trial for a dramatic protest in Taoyuan, led the march. As we marched through central Taipei, the demonstration wove around the Japanese-owned Mitsukoshi Department Store, past the recently renamed February 28 Memorial Park, and finally arrived at its destination, the Presidential Building.

As soon as we arrived at the Presidential Building, we were surrounded by shielded policemen and soldiers. Security forces far outnumbered the protesters. Union leaders gave speeches, and one group staged a short theatrical performance. They enacted a courtroom scene, with a judge and executioner in traditional Chinese costume. They put a worker on trial and called attention to how the trial was rigged because the capitalists had the money and power to rig the system of justice in their favor. Suddenly, however, the workers took over the courtroom and executed the judge, at which point the play was over, and the crowd sang the "Internationale" hymn of the working class.

After the play, more union leaders gave speeches and outlined immediate demands for political change. Chief among their demands was a national labor court, dominated by unions, to mediate labor disputes. They had drafted a petition to President Lee Teng-hui and asked for a representative of the government to come out and accept the letter. When it became apparent that no one was willing to come out and accept the petition, a group of workers began to agitate for storming the Presidential Building and called out for Lee Teng-hui to resign. The security forces gathered in closer around the demonstrators, their shields raised and batons in hand as if they were prepared for battle. After fifteen tense minutes, a member of the government finally came out of the Presidential Building, escorted by police officers, and accepted the petition. He spoke for a few minutes, arguing that the government would listen to workers' concerns. The security forces rolled back and the crowd dispersed.

The Taiwanese labor movement is small, but it has been growing since martial law was lifted in 1987. The symbolism used in the demonstration, including prison uniforms for all of the demonstrators and a play showing the diametric opposition between labor and capital in a staged courtroom setting, clearly showed that some workers perceive their collective interests to be

Figure 7.2   Workers' demonstration: a labor protest in front of the Presidential Building, May Day 1997.

opposed to that of the factory owners. The selection of a Chinese gown for the oppressive judge was a potent symbol of Chinese Nationalist Party oppression. Strong deployment of state force at the event also revealed that the state considers workers to be a potentially dangerous source of opposition. Unions organize such peaceful demonstrations several times a year to express their dissatisfaction with labor relations in Taiwan. Yet May Day demonstrations are not the only form of worker resistance in Taiwan.

INCIDENTS OF WORKER RESISTANCE

The most direct forms of class struggle are what Scott (1985) termed "everyday forms of resistance" on factory premises. One common form of resistance is gossip about the bosses (Hsiung 1996: 139) and criticism of their business practices. By engaging in such discussions, workers assert their own power through knowledge of the labor process and critical assessments of management decisions. One worker complained to me, for example, that the owner had invested too much money in expensive imported equipment and thus lacked the funds to purchase raw hides. As a result, he had to rely on subcontracts from larger factories. As such orders are undependable, the tannery alternates between long slack periods with no work and rush periods when workers are expected to do long hours of overtime. Rather than describing the situation in Marxist terms as an oppressive labor regime, however, that worker explained it as a foolish management decision, asserting his own knowledge and implying that he knew more about the tannery business than his boss.

Sometimes workers take more direct forms of resistance. If they are unhappy with work conditions, they may intentionally slow down work or intentionally make mistakes. The technically complex tasks of tanning make leather factories relatively easy to sabotage. As one boss-wife told me, "If the workers are unhappy, they sabotage the labor process by using too many or too little chemicals at certain points in the tanning process and ruin the leather. So I have to work hard to keep them happy."

Organized resistance is less common but can assume dramatic proportions. In December 1986, the owner of Taoyuan's Lien-hu Garment Factory moved production to China and closed the Taiwanese factory without giving workers the severance pay guaranteed by law. In protest, the aforementioned group of eighty-five female workers risked their lives and attracted media attention by demonstrating on the train tracks and disrupting railroad service for over an hour. Cases such as this reveal the ability of Taiwanese workers to resist when pushed too far. Labor disputes, in fact, have been on the increase ever since martial law was lifted in 1987. The main causes of labor disputes have been contentious labor contracts, followed by wage disputes and problems with occupational hazards (Executive Yuan Council of Labor Affairs 1995: 66–67).

Taiwanese sociologists have demonstrated that Taiwanese workers do possess class identity, even if it has not led to violent opposition to capitalism as Marx had anticipated. Wu Nai-teh found that 77 percent of manual workers identified with the working class, suggesting that Taiwanese workers are no less class conscious than workers in Western countries (Wu 1996: 88). Wu also found no correlation between class identity and size of firms. Working in small firms seems not to influence class identity, even if it does seem to reduce oppositional attitudes (Wu 1996: 95). Because Taiwanese workers have a high level of working-class identity but a low level of anti-capitalist attitudes, Wu concluded that class in Taiwan is a "hollow identity" with little impact on political opposition (Wu 1996: 101).

Wang Chen-huan similarly concluded that Taiwanese workers perceive themselves as belonging to a unified class but are not opposed to capitalism (Wang 1993: 214). One possible reason may be that there are good opportunities for social mobility in Taiwan. Even working-class Taiwanese believe it is possible for their children to attend good universities and move into a different social class. As seen in the narratives of tanners, it has indeed been possible for workers to leave their factories and eventually become bosses themselves.

Most opposition thus tends to be toward specific companies, rather than against capitalism as a political and economic system. In order to understand why, it is important to look first at the role of the state, and second, at how Taiwanese bosses gain consent on the factory floor.

LABOR RELATIONS IN AN AUTOCRATIC STATE

On the front line against communism in East Asia, the Chinese Nationalist Party took several measures to prevent the emergence of class struggle in Taiwan. One of the most radical and most successful policies used to fend off communism was the land-reform program (see Chapter 2). Land reform had a major impact on the industrialization of Taiwan, as many rural people used their newly acquired land to build small manufacturing workshops. By giving land to so many people, the Chinese Nationalist Party slowed the development of a landless proletariat, which Marx saw as a necessary precondition for class formation and class struggle. Those smallholders who gained property through land reform were much like the peasants described in Marx's *The Eighteenth Brumaire,* who did not develop class consciousness due to the appeasement measures taken by the state (Marx 1963).

In case such indirect measures were insufficient, the state intervened directly in labor relations. Following the massacres that came in the wake of the February 28 incident, the security apparatus of the Chinese Nationalist Party completely obliterated autonomous labor unions. Taiwanese sociologist Wang Chen-huan argued that the party-state further averted the development of class consciousness and a radical labor movement through two related policies. First, the government took a state corporatist stand toward labor, regulating wages, insurance, and benefits in ways that sometimes benefited labor. The government established state-controlled labor unions and set up local institutions for workers. Workers' Recreation Centers, established all over Taiwan, still provide sports facilities, gathering space, and even hostel accommodations for use by Taiwanese workers. These institutions express state control over the working class but also have the effect of institutionalizing it. Because workers are encouraged by such state institutions to identify themselves as workers, a strong class identity has developed in Taiwan.

Class identity, however, did not lead to class conflict, as the state suppressed autonomous labor organization. Each large factory had a union controlled by Chinese Nationalist Party cadres, who often acted in direct collusion with management. Under martial law, independent labor unions were outlawed. In fact, inciting a strike could potentially incur the death penalty (Arrigo 1985). Undercover security forces worked in factories to prevent labor conflict and to weed out potential autonomous labor organizers. Workers were thus understandably afraid to take direct collective action in protest of abuse or poor conditions (Wang 1993). The use, or even the threat, of force to prevent labor unrest implies that there probably was a strong working-class consciousness and a fear of communism during the early decades of Chinese Nationalist rule in Taiwan. Otherwise, Chiang Kai-shek would never have perceived the need to crush unions and place undercover security agents in factories.

Economist Joseph Lee saw three stages in the evolution of labor relations in Taiwan. The first stage, from 1946 to 1960, was characterized by authoritarian industrial relations and repressive government policy. The second stage, from 1961 to 1980, was one of paternalistic industrial relations and inactive government policy. The third stage, from 1981 to the mid-1990s, consisted of modern industrial relations and an active government labor policy. During this period, the state slowly became more pro-labor, unions became more powerful, and industrial relations became increasingly formalized (Lee 1995: 89).

The strongest pro-labor state action was the implementation of the Basic Labor Standards Law (LSL) in 1984. In 1987, the government created a cabinet-level Council of Labor Affairs to enforce this law and handle labor disputes. The LSL stipulated a minimum wage, welfare benefits, and minimum labor standards, all with the intent of protecting workers. The law, however, dissatisfied workers and capitalists alike. Labor was dissatisfied because the law initially covered only certain occupations and would only be enforced in companies with more than thirty workers. In 1998, the law was expanded to cover all occupations. The focus of labor organization in June 1998 was no longer factory workers but bank employees. In June 1998, bank employees in Taipei protested because a number of large banks refused to enforce the legal limits on women working at night.

Capitalists were dissatisfied with the LSL because it raised labor costs by as much as 30 percent (Lee 1995: 105). Companies thus responded to the LSL by automating production, moving labor-intensive production abroad, hiring foreign workers, and subcontracting production to small workshops. Small firms and satellite companies in subcontracting networks were the main violators of the LSL (Lee 1995: 105). The law, in fact, was routinely ignored in small factories and subcontracting workshops, especially in regard to overtime and holidays. When I noted that workers in one tannery were working on a legal holiday, for example, the owner merely remarked, "We have to pay them for holidays anyway, so they might as well work."

The watershed moment in Taiwanese labor relations occurred in 1987, when martial law was lifted. Autonomous labor unions and strikes were legalized, making it possible for an autonomous labor movement to emerge. One leading labor organization was the Taiwanese Labor Front, an autonomous labor association composed of labor activists from autonomous trade unions and intellectuals. It was initially established on May 1, 1984, as the Taiwan Labor Legal Assistance Association (TLLAA). Under martial law, the organization was not allowed to directly organize labor or incite strikes and thus

Figure 7.3   A Labor Protest. The sign reads, "Blood and sweat money."

focused on providing free legal aid to workers. After martial law was lifted, the TLLAA was reorganized as the Taiwan Labor Movement Assistance Association, designed to help workers form autonomous unions and train union leaders. In 1992, it was renamed the Taiwanese Labor Front, becoming a grassroots organization promoting the labor movement and labor reform law.

At the time this research was done, Taiwanese manufacturers had the inertia of history working on their side. Autonomous labor unions had recently been legalized, but unionization was slow. Since the state took such a paternalistic stance toward labor, exemplified through the Basic Labor Standards Law and government-sponsored labor service centers to regulate workers' complaints, the demand for labor unions was reduced, even as legal space for them expanded. Like the French peasants described by Marx, the workers of Taiwan have been largely appeased by the state. At the level of individual factories, moreover, Taiwanese bosses are adept at gaining consent in a variety of ways. These include the employment of cultural ideology, the use of recruitment techniques that inhibit unified class consciousness, and the outright purchase of consent.

THE CULTURAL POLITICS OF PRODUCTION

When discussing their own culture, many Taiwanese people take pride in a "human touch," or *jin-cheng-bi,* which Taiwanese people bring to everyday transactions. Many view this human touch as a uniquely Taiwanese characteristic, whereas others label it as Chinese. In school textbooks, it is taught that this "human touch" is a product of the Chinese Confucian tradition. *Jin-cheng-bi* can be as simple as asking people questions about their personal life in order to express concern. It can also involve the sharing of time, eating together, or exchanging small gifts.

Jin-cheng-bi provides a personal touch in what might otherwise be impersonal market exchanges. An example would be the relationship between Tainan businesswoman Ngo Ting-ing and a young loan officer at her bank. Although their relationship was originally a market relationship between a bank officer and his client, it eventually grew into friendship due to Ngo Ting-ing's ability to use *jin-cheng-bi*. When that loan officer's girlfriend left him, for example, he immediately called on Ngo Ting-ing for advice. She invited him to coffee and gave him advice on how to gain and keep a girlfriend. Taiwanese people are well aware, however, that *jin-cheng-bi* can be manipulated for personal gain. Another loan officer, who introduced me to a leather tanning client and then left to take care of other business, warned me not to accept any dinner invitation for the two of us afterward. He was afraid that they might use the occasion to try to negotiate better conditions on their loan.

A related concept is *kam-cheng*, which refers to an emotional bond. It can refer to the close emotional attachment between lovers, or husband and wife. It can also refer to more mundane personal relations. One Taiwanese friend, for example, explained that my tendency to eat in the same restaurant was a result of the *kam-cheng* that existed between me and the proprietor. When someone gets along well with another person, they say that their *kam-cheng* is good. *Kam-cheng*, however, can be broken with serious consequences. In describing the breakdown of her business partnership, for example, one entrepreneur said that the *kam-cheng* between the partners had broken down due to constant arguments about the telephone bills. Without sufficient emotional attachment, they felt they could no longer do business together.

Kam-cheng is especially important in class relations. As Morton Fried noted in his study of China, *kam-cheng* "is the primary institutionalized technique by which class differences are reduced between non-related persons" (Fried 1969 [1953]: 103). Successful factory owners are skilled at using *kam-cheng* with workers to manage labor relations. As sociologist Ping-Chun Hsiung pointed out, bosses invest a lot of time and effort in cultivating good will with employees and developing personal relations with them (Hsiung 1996: 133).

In conversations about labor relations, tanners strongly emphasized how strong *kam-cheng* is in their own tanneries. Bosses are expected to become involved in the personal lives of their employees by giving personal favors in times of need. They contribute financially to expensive family events such as marriages and funerals. Many male workers even expect their bosses to foot the bill for an occasional visit to a prostitute. Cultivating good will with employees, however, pays off in the long run. Because it makes workers feel emotionally indebted to their bosses, it can be used to convince workers to stay with a company and to put in long overtime hours when production needs demand it. Some workers, in fact, disguise their employment status by referring to their work in factories as "helping" *(bangmang)*.

Some workers prefer an employment relationship that encourages a personal relationship between employer and employee. In a survey of workers in one tannery, I found that twelve out of sixty-eight workers (17.6 percent) preferred to work in family firms. The respondents who said they preferred small family firms were all older women who said they preferred family firms because they were better at cultivating *kam-cheng*.

Kam-cheng, however, can also be used by management as a political tool. In my interviews with tannery owners, I asked if their factories are unionized. I found that none were unionized, although some larger tanneries had welfare societies that organized social events and helped workers in times of need. Tanners often claimed that they had no need for unions because they maintained good *kam-cheng* with their workers and didn't need assistance in labor relations. Some claimed that *kam-cheng* was a special Taiwanese trait that had allowed them to avoid the confrontational, union-based labor relations of the West. Some of them emphasized this to me because they feared I might actually be a labor organizer from a foreign labor rights organization.[1]

The human touch of maintaining long-term personal relations is an effective way to do business and manage labor anywhere. In Taiwan, *kam-cheng* and *jin-cheng-bi* make up an effective cultural argument because people believe they are Taiwanese cultural traits. Yet the political implications of such arguments must be rendered visible. Whether they are labeled as Taiwanese or Chinese, in the factory context they are used to control labor and to justify the absence of labor unions in individual factories. *Kam-cheng*, however, is clearly insufficient in itself to control labor. If such cultural institutions were enough to prevent labor unrest, the Chinese Nationalist Party state would never have needed to take the anti-labor measures described above. Taiwanese capitalists are well aware of the limitations of cultural ideology in the workplace and employ other means to gain consent. Just as the selection of the right hides is central to manufacturing leather, the recruitment of the right workers is central to gaining consent.

RECRUITMENT TACTICS:
FINDING A DOCILE LABOR FORCE

Finding labor is one of the biggest challenges faced by Taiwanese leather tanners. Older tanners complain that Taiwanese people have become lazy and are no longer willing to do hard work. Only a generation ago, jobs were so scarce that people were willing to take any job, even strenuous work in a leather tannery. Many people, in fact, had to bribe foremen in factories in order to get one of the few manufacturing jobs available. Now, however, labor is so scarce that factories have trouble finding workers. As one tanner said:

> The Taiwanese don't want to do leather tanning. Nowadays, the Taiwanese like to dress well and work in offices. But tanning is smelly, difficult, and heavy. Most of all, it smells really bad. Hides are like human skins, with veins, blood, and fat. They can be infected with worms, they attract insects, and they go moldy. Tanning is also a heavy job, since the wet cowhides weigh a lot. It is a very strenuous job.

The work is not only dirty and smelly but also strenuous and demanding. It can also pose potential health problems. One tannery owner I interviewed, for example, had contracted a fungal lung infection from moldy cowhides, despite the fact that he had no direct contact with the hides. Production workers, on the other hand, are exposed to hides and chemicals for eight or more hours a day. In the busy seasons, they are expected to work overtime, often late into the night. Tanners report that most new workers only last a few months before leaving for other jobs, and some leave after working for only a few hours. Those that can get accustomed to the hard work and unpleasant odors, however, usually stay for ten to twenty years or until retirement.

Tanneries must therefore resort to a number of recruiting tactics in order to find a docile labor force willing to do the strenuous work of tanning. Primary among those tactics are the recruitment of rural labor, elderly labor, female labor, and foreign labor. Workers from these groups are perceived to be more obedient than other workers. The fact that they are so different from one another, moreover, inhibits the creation of a unified class consciousness that could lead to confrontation against capitalism.

Many tanners said they chose a rural location because it was easier to find workers in the countryside. Some said that rural people were more industrious workers because they were already accustomed to the strenuous work of agriculture. The higher risk of unemployment also made rural workers more docile. One pigskin tannery, for example, moved production from an industrial park outside the city of Kaohsiung to rural Yunlin County because it was easier to control rural labor. One of the female shareholders in the company, in charge of labor control, compared Kaohsiung and Yunlin workers: "Kaohsiung workers are harder to control because there are so many factories that they'll just change jobs if they are unhappy. The workers here don't leave because they don't have much choice but going back to farming or sitting at home and doing nothing at all."

Another common tactic is to hire older workers for unskilled jobs in the labor process of tanning. When asked about the age of the labor force, tanners usually characterized their Taiwanese workers as "old." Many of them, in

Figure 7.4   Older women working in a tannery.

fact, employed teams of older women, whom they call *obaasan* (Japanese for "grandmother") to work in dry tanning. One tanner estimated that about two-thirds of tannery workers are over forty years old. In my own visits to tanneries, I had the same impression, as I saw a lot of older men and women working in both the dry and wet tanning process. In the tannery where I worked briefly, for example, the only young workers were a handful of temporary migrants from Thailand. Tanners attribute this to the laziness of young people. As one explained:

> Taiwan prospered because the Holo and Hakka peoples were hard-working and industrious, but now the young people are lazy, especially young men. The older generation succeeded because of their hard work, but now they don't want their children to lead the same bitter lives that they experienced. It's a big problem. So we hire a lot of old women, because they are still very industrious.

Older women are relatively easy to control, as they have few other employment options available. Moreover, they often work only to supplement the income of their families. It is common in Taiwan for elderly people in poor families to do poorly remunerated manual labor, such as collecting recyclable materials from garbage, selling chewing gum on the street, or working in factories. They contribute their meager earnings to the family budget and relieve some of the financial burden of younger family members. These older workers perceive themselves not as permanent members of a working class but as needy individuals working temporarily to help their families. They are sometimes seen as deserving of pity. As one informant remarked, "Those factory *obaasan* are all mothers of unfilial sons. Their sons are all convicts and gamblers and don't support their elderly mothers."

Some studies show that women have lower class consciousness than men (Wu 1996: 91), a conclusion consistent with tanners' observations that women are more industrious and cause less trouble than men. Tanners believe that women are more docile than men, and thus they hire large numbers of women. Sixty-eight tanneries provided data on workers. They employed 2,508 men and 1,756 women, divided by gender and nationality as shown in Table 7.1.

Table 7.1   Gender and Nationality of Tanning Labor Force, 1996–1997

	Taiwanese	Foreign	Total
Male	1,761	747	2,508
Female	1,720	36	1,756
Total	3,481	783	4,264

Source: Interviews with tannery owners, 1996–97.

From these statistics, it is apparent that leather tanning is not exclusively a male occupation. Men dominate the workforce, but primarily because of the large number of foreign men employed in the industry. Almost all of the foreign tanners are men, more because of the gendered division of labor as constructed by the employment agencies than due to dynamics within the tanneries. Among Filipino guest workers, for example, men usually go to Taiwan as factory workers and women as housekeepers. If we look at the gender composition of the Taiwanese labor force alone, Taiwanese men and women work in tanneries in about equal numbers.

Men and women, however, do not get equal pay. Women earn around NT$15,000 (US$476) per month, and men earn around NT$25,000 (US$794) per month. Tannery owners justify lower pay for women with the fact that women work in dry tanning, which is considered to be an easier job.

The assumption made by tanners that women are more docile workers than men is probably untrue, as is evidenced by the women protesters in Taoyuan mentioned above. More important than gender is the fact that most women working in leather tanneries are *obaasan,* or older women. As mentioned above, these women identify themselves not as members of a united working class but merely as individuals contributing as they can to their household budgets. These older women's social identities as older women and mothers mask their class identities and discourage them from participating in a broader labor movement. A unified class identity is further restrained by the strategic use of foreign workers.

FOREIGN LABOR: MASKING CLASS IDENTITY

By the end of the 1980s, many Taiwanese companies were moving abroad to solve the problem of high wages and scarce labor. In an effort to keep production jobs in Taiwan, the government began permitting the use of foreign labor in 1990. The government strictly regulates the use of foreign labor; only firms in targeted industries and of a minimum size are permitted to hire foreign workers. Leather is one of the specified industries, and all but a few tanneries meet the minimum-size requirements.

As Table 7.1 shows, nationality is now important in the organization of labor in Taiwanese tanneries, as more than 18 percent of the workforce is foreign labor. By far the largest group of foreign workers comes from Thailand. In 1996–1997, the sixty-eight tanneries in my study employed a total of 648 Thais, 93 Filipinos, 39 Indonesians, 2 Indian technicians, and at least 1 mainland Chinese who crossed over to Taiwan illegally from Fujian.[2] Among the Taiwanese workers, ethnicity did not appear to be an important variable. In my survey of workers, sixty-six workers identified themselves as native Taiwanese, but only one as a Mainlander, one as overseas Chinese, and none as Hakka or aboriginal.

Both gender and nationality influence the social organization of labor in the tanneries. Generally, men are concentrated in the wet tanning stages, and women in the dry tanning stages. Foreign workers also are concentrated in the wet tanning stages. The most unpleasant tasks, as well as much of the overtime work, are assigned to foreign workers. Taiwanese workers are increasingly unwilling to work nights, as it interferes with their family lives. Taiwanese firms thus rely more and more on foreign labor for overtime and night shifts. Overtime work is dangerous, as long hours weaken a worker's ability to concentrate on manual tasks, thus increasing the risk of injury. When production orders rise, most tanneries push their workers as far as possible. As one tanner said:

> We've been working long hours since the New Year, when we fell behind on production due to the long holiday. And foreign orders still pour in! The Taiwanese workers only work until midnight, and the foreigners work until three or four in the morning. The bosses stay up with them in order to push the production through. We haven't been taking any breaks at all, not even on Sundays.

Figure 7.5   Foreign worker: a Filipino worker takes care of the tanning drums.

Foreign workers are rarely given technical jobs, for two reasons. First, they are allowed to stay in the factories for only two years, so tanneries are reluctant to train them to do the more challenging jobs only to see them leave and have to retrain new workers. Second, there is often a language barrier between the tanners and their foreign workers, so it is difficult to train them to do technical tasks. With those two constraints, most employers simply put foreign workers in the technically less complex, but more dangerous, manual tasks of the tannery.

Workers from different countries have varying reputations among leather tanners, although all of them are perceived as more industrious than the Taiwanese. Since Filipino workers are accustomed to labor unions and confrontational labor relations, they protest when working conditions are poor. Thai workers are perceived as more diligent and less likely to protest. Indonesians are reputedly slow but honest and dependable workers. Religion is an important factor when dealing with foreign workers. Most Filipino workers are Roman Catholic and often demand to have Sunday free so that they may attend Mass. Thai workers, however, are Buddhist, like many Taiwanese, and thus have no fixed days of worship. Therefore, they are available for overtime work on Sundays, unlike Filipinos.

Tanners that hire foreign workers insist that the practice does not save tanneries a lot of money in monthly wages. This is because the Taiwanese state established wage guidelines for foreign workers in order to avert increased unemployment among the local Taiwanese population. In 1996, tanneries were required to pay NT$15,800 (US$502) to NT$23,700 (US$752) a month to skilled workers and NT$13,300 (US$422) to NT$19,900 (US$632) to unskilled workers. In my study, I found that foreign workers earned about NT$18,000 (US$571) per month. Since tanneries were also required to provide foreign workers with food, dormitory accommodations, and insurance, each foreign worker cost a tannery about NT$25,000 (US$794) per month. Foreign workers were thus slightly more expensive than local workers at the time of this study, but only if measured in terms of *monthly wages* rather than actual production.

More important than the stipulated monthly wage is the fact that foreign workers are less likely than Taiwanese to protest the exploitive use of overtime work. Since foreign workers are in Taiwan for only short two- or three-year contracts, their main goal is to make as much money as possible and then return home. They thus welcome the overtime hours that Taiwanese people often refuse. During the busiest seasons, when tanneries add night shifts, most tanners send their Taiwanese workers home and keep their foreign workers laboring through the night. The norm for foreign workers is twelve hours a day, whereas Taiwanese workers work only eight. Even foreign workers resent such work conditions and told me so during lunch breaks in two tanneries. They tolerate the long hours and hard work only because their contracts are temporary and wages are much higher than in their own countries. Furthermore, they are not free to break their contracts and move on to other factories. Taiwanese workers, on the other hand, are likely to quit their jobs and move to other factories if pressed too hard.

Not all tanneries hire foreign labor, however. Due to negative stereotypes of Southeast Asian workers, some tanneries refuse to hire foreign workers, believing that they will drink too much or get into fights. Whether they hire foreign workers or not, tanners describe Southeast Asian workers as diseased, "backward," and prone to crime (Lin 2004: 111–128). Discipline, in fact, is one of the main tropes used by tanners who hire foreign labor. As one tanner said:

> Foreign labor is important. Without foreign labor, even more factories would move abroad. But it's hard to manage foreign workers. We start out by being strict, but then we eventually let up. Some factories are like the military, doing things like not letting workers leave the factory at night. But I prefer to cultivate *kam-cheng*. If workers have *kam-cheng* with the boss, they won't go out and make trouble.

This unusual mix of workers is probably enough in itself to slow the formation of a unified working-class identity in Taiwan. The young foreign men of the wet tanning sections and the elderly Taiwanese women of the dry tanning sections come into the tanneries with entirely different interests and do not even share a common language with which to discuss labor problems. Unless Taiwanese labor unions can better organize such diverse groups of workers and contribute to the formation of a class identity that transcends national difference, the probability of unified protest is low.

Purchasing Consent: Wages and Benefits

Not only is consent gained through cultural politics and the shrewd choice of a docile labor force, but in a capitalist economy, consent is also purchased on the labor market. Through a "wage-effort bargain," capitalists persuade workers to produce by offering increases in wages and other benefits (Shieh 1997: 13). For over thirty years, industrial wages steadily rose in Taiwan, giving Taiwanese workers unprecedented prosperity. Taiwanese tanners were adequately remunerated for their labor through the 1990s. Workers in leather tanneries earned between NT$15,000 (US$476) and NT$25,000 (US$794) a month, and skilled technicians earned around NT$40,000 (US$1,270). Taking overtime pay into consideration, the highest-paid leather tanners in Taiwan could make as much as NT$80,000 (US$2540) a month.

From 1965 to 1975, Taiwan's labor productivity increased by 5.19 percent annually, while the real wage rate increased 5.91 percent. From 1976 to 1986, productivity rose 5.27 percent annually, while the real wage rate increased 5.3 percent. Over that twenty-year period, real wages in Taiwan grew 150 percent, a real wage increase that is the envy of the rest of the world (Lee 1995: 98–99). In interviews, labor organizers told me that wages were high enough in Taiwan that wages were not a useful rallying point for union organization. Instead, unions focused their attention on working conditions and issues such as retirement pay.

In addition to wages, workers receive numerous other benefits. Bosses often embed these benefits in a paternalistic ideology in order to nurture *kamcheng* with workers. Most of the tanneries I studied, for example, provided workers with financial aid for weddings, funerals, and other major life-cycle expenses. Many of them organized social events, such as day trips to local scenic areas, sports events, or karaoke singing. Those that could afford it even took workers on group tours to Hong Kong and Southeast Asia. In large tanneries, these benefits were distributed through factory welfare societies, which many tanners argued constitute an adequate substitute for unions.

Almost all of the tanners I interviewed reported giving annual bonuses in the form of "red envelopes" stuffed with money at the Chinese New Year, often equivalent to a month's wages. Although tanners usually perceived red envelopes as a form of profit-sharing that should be tied to productivity, workers usually saw it as a customary right and often compared their bonuses with those received by workers in other factories. Bosses that gave smaller bonuses than others were perceived as stingy. Ninety-six percent of Taiwanese manufacturing enterprises reported giving annual bonuses (Executive Yuan Council of Labor Affairs 1995: 242). In a study conducted by the Council of Labor Affairs, 57 percent of manufacturing workers found their annual bonuses to be "fair and reasonable," 23 percent found them "acceptable," and only 1.52 percent found them "too low" (Executive Yuan Council of Labor Affairs 1995: 250–251).

Because workers compared benefits with friends and family, and labor mobility was high, companies had to compete on the basis of benefits in order to recruit and keep workers. As one tanner reported:

> In Taiwanese firms, if the benefits are good, employees will introduce their family and friends to come there to work. Employees have faith in a company only if the benefits are good. Then they want their friends and family members to work there too. Before, we couldn't keep up with the number of people being introduced. Now that the benefits are less generous than before, our employees rarely introduce people to us, except for the relatively easy jobs.

Until at least the 1990s, workers could claim larger portions of an increasing economic pie. Workers received reasonable wages and benefits, and unemployment was extremely low. From 1985 to 1994, unemployment remained between 1 and 2 percent, highly enviable rates compared to Canada and Western Europe (Executive Yuan Council of Labor Affairs 1995: 594). From January to November of 1997, when this research was conducted, the average monthly unemployment rate was 2.74 percent, the highest since 1986 (*Zili Zaobao*, December 24, 1997). The high availability of jobs meant that workers were able to change jobs rather than join unions or resort to collective action when they were unsatisfied with working conditions. This contributed to Taiwan's notably high labor mobility rate (Lee 1995: 108). In such an economy, capitalists had to compete to recruit workers, and labor was a seller's market.[3]

DISCUSSION

Wage labor is so common in Taiwan, even in so-called family firms, that any study of Taiwanese manufacturing is incomplete without a discussion of labor relations. Most evidence, from the results of sociological studies to the growing incidence of collective labor disputes, indicates that Taiwanese workers identify themselves as members of a working class. This class identity, moreover, has been part of state ideology and has been crystallized through such institutions as state-supported trade unions and workers recreation centers. The strongest evidence of Taiwanese working-class consciousness is found in the actions of the Chinese Nationalist Party and its state apparatus. During the forty years of martial law, the government feared Taiwanese workers so much that inciting a strike was punishable by death.

Since the end of martial law in 1987, autonomous labor unions and even strikes have been permitted. Labor disputes have risen since then, probably due to a backlog of complaints workers were afraid to address under martial law. Due to the rapid expansion of the economy in the past thirty years, however, the living standard of workers has improved dramatically. In such an economic environment, there has been little incentive for widespread collective action against capitalism. Workers have little trust in either their bosses or the state and would likely support stronger labor unions. However, in times of low unemployment, a labor shortage, and high labor mobility, it is easier for individual workers to gain better working conditions by moving elsewhere than it is to organize collective action.

It is difficult as well to mobilize a collective identity as workers, when class identity is masked by the national and ethnic differences between workers. Within tanneries and other factories, workers of different nationalities have very little social contact with one another and even have difficulty communicating due to the language barrier. Although production managers can often give work orders and instructions in English, there is little chance of communication between the migrants and their Taiwanese co-workers except in rare cases where migrants learn some Taiwanese. Taiwanese workers, moreover, share with their bosses a sense of national superiority over "backward" workers from Southeast Asia. In Taiwan, nationalism thus masks class identity. Further trends toward the internationalization of production make the creation of a unified working-class identity even less likely.

Taiwan's economic picture changed, however, when in 1990 the Taiwanese government legalized Taiwanese investment in China. As a result, Taiwanese capitalists began shifting investment to the more favorable conditions on the mainland. By 1993, Taiwan already had 8,360 investment projects in China, for a total value of US$7,905,670,000. That placed Taiwanese direct foreign investment in China second only to Hong Kong and far ahead of both Japan and the United States. Taiwan, in fact, accounted for 8.51 percent of China's direct foreign investment, without counting investment made through third-party intermediaries (Schive 1995: 96). In this context, many labor organizers have become alarmed at the "hollowing out" of manufacturing in Taiwan, a change that could increase unemployment and subsequently reduce the relative power of workers in the economy. The influence of Taiwanese investment in China on the island's national identity, however, remains to be explored. That is the topic of the next chapter.

Notes

1. I remain skeptical about a cultural chasm between a *kam-cheng*-oriented Taiwan and a union-based West. Taiwan in 1994 had 3,706 unions, accounting for 36 percent of the total workforce. The manufacturing sector had 983 unions with 398,000 members, or 16 percent of the workforce (Executive Yuan Council of Labor Affairs 1995: 65). In the United States, by contrast, barely 10 percent of the private sector workforce and 14.5 percent of the total workforce was unionized in the same year.

2. There may be more illegal Fujianese workers, but factory owners are unlikely to reveal that fact to a foreign researcher.

3. In April 2004, the unemployment rate was 4.36 percent. If unemployment continues to rise, labor conditions may worsen.

CHAPTER EIGHT

CROSS-STRAIT INVESTMENT AND NATIONAL IDENTITY

Issues of national identity have been central to the study of Taiwan in the 1990s and 2000s within the disciplines of anthropology (Brown 2004; Katz and Rubinstein 2003; Lu 2002), political science (Corcuff 2002a; Wachman 1994), and related fields. Taiwanese identity was originally an *ethnic* identity based on historically constituted boundaries between the Mainlanders who arrived with the Chinese Nationalist Party in the 1940s and the Native Taiwanese who had already been living on Taiwan. As the agent of Chinese domination of Taiwan, the Chinese Nationalist Party long oppressed any signs of Taiwanese aspirations toward independence, including Taiwanese language and the study of Taiwanese history. Instead, the Chinese Nationalist government justified their rule of Taiwan with the "founding myth" (Wachman 1994: 131) that Taiwan is part of China and its people essentially Chinese. Some of those who opposed Chinese domination of Taiwan were imprisoned on Green Island. Walls of the prison were painted with the slogan "Taiwan's independence is Taiwan's poison" to remind them daily of the reason for their imprisonment. Most Taiwanese people thus limited their opposition to the Chinese National Party to private conversation until martial law was lifted in 1987.

What I observed in the tanneries of Taiwan was the assertion of a local Taiwanese identity at the end of the first decade of democratization. It is important to emphasize that this form of Taiwanese identity was initially a reaction of the island's Holo Taiwanese to Chinese Nationalist control of Taiwan and subsequent Mainlander domination of society. Even the early struggles of the

Figure 8.1   Prison walls. Some who opposed Chiang's rule were imprisoned on Green Island. A slogan on the wall reads, "Taiwan independence equals Taiwan poison. Communism equals bankruptcy."

Taiwanese independence movement were oriented toward independence of Taiwan from the *Republic of China* and had little to say about the Communist regime in China. The origins of Taiwanese identity were thus unrelated to events in the *People's Republic of China*. The "other" that spurred early Taiwanese nationalism was the regime that arrived with Chiang Kai-shek in 1945.

It was only in the 1980s, with the beginning of contacts across the Taiwan Strait, that a civic form of national identity started to emerge from Taiwanese ethnic identity. In 1987, the ban was lifted on travel from Taiwan to China. Taiwanese tourists and investors started traveling to China in great numbers, and the leather industry was one of the first to be integrated with business counterparts on the mainland. By 1994, horse and cow leather goods had become Taiwan's tenth largest export to China (Schive 1995: 30). Most of this consisted of cowhides tanned in Taiwan and destined for Taiwanese-owned shoe factories in Guangzhou or Fujian—trade engaged in by those described in this book.

In this chapter, I examine whether investment in China has increased or decreased identification with China and Chinese culture. In the long run, Taiwanese business involvement in China could influence questions of identity in two different ways that are not mutually exclusive. It could integrate the economies and make them increasingly interdependent. It could also reinforce separate national identities, however, as Taiwanese investors discover differences between their own lifestyles and those of people in China. The discovery of difference could increase perceptions of Taiwan and China as distinct national entities. The lived experience of carrying a passport and traveling internationally has in itself a strong influence on national identity as well.

When I conducted my research in 1996–1998, Taiwanese tanners had already invested not only in China but also in other foreign countries. Out of the sixty-eight tanneries for which I have full data, twenty-five had already made investments abroad, in at least one country, for a total of twenty-nine foreign investment projects. By far, the favored investment destination was China, as twenty of those tanneries had invested there. Six invested in Southeast Asia, two in New Zealand, and one in Canada. Most tanners investing outside of Taiwan have moved production to China, especially the heavily polluting wet tanning stages of the labor process. The two tanneries described below are typical examples of factories that have moved production to China.

Dividing Up the Tanning Process

Lau Hung-chi slowly sipped at a cup of Chinese herbal medicine during our interview. He had just come back from his tannery in Guangdong Province of southern China, where he had caught a fungal infection in his lungs due to exposure to infected hides. When the cough seemed untreatable, he returned to Taiwan for medical treatment, which gave me a chance to interview this otherwise busy entrepreneur. The history of his tannery is typical of those who invest in China and reflects the difficulties of the Taiwanese industry as a whole.

Mr. Lau began his narrative with a history of the tannery, which was originally founded by his father, Lau Se-hong. His grandfather died at a young age, leaving the thirteen-year-old Lau Se-hong to help his mother take care of the younger children. As they lacked the financial means to send him to school, he began work after his father's death in a Tainan shoe factory. When he got older, he went into the leather trade, buying finished leather from tanneries and selling it to leather products factories. When he saved up enough capital, he bought a leather tannery, speculating that it would be even more profitable than trade. Since he had never worked in a tannery, however, he hired an elderly splitter as master of the shop and learned the technical aspects of the trade from him. He, in turn, taught his sons how to tan leather.

The tannery has by now made a transition to the second generation. All of the management and stockholders are family members, but no relatives work directly in the labor process. The father, Lau Se-hong, is still nominally the CEO, but he and his wife no longer actually participate in tannery operations. The three sons have divided the responsibilities among themselves and their wives. Lau Hung-chi, the eldest son, is thirty-three years old and a high school graduate. He oversees the Guangdong plant but also works as a technician and salesman, as dictated by the immediate needs of the tannery. His wife is an accountant and administrator. His younger brother works in the tannery as production manager. His wife handles accounting and administrative tasks. The youngest brother is still in college. He studies environmental engineering, a specialty they hope will help the family tannery make a transition to less polluting tanning techniques.

Their reasons for moving to China reflect the concerns of an industry adjusting to rapid change within Taiwan. Like other tanneries, the Lau family tannery faces two crucial problems. The first is a labor shortage, which is so critical that family members must participate in the labor process of tanning when a worker doesn't show up for work. Company welfare is good, insisted Lau. The tannery offers workers an annual bonus, subsidizes an annual company trip, helps pay for marriage and funeral expenses, and aids workers when a child is sick. Nonetheless, it is hard to find workers. Most of their employees are old. They have trouble finding younger workers, since few young people want to endure the hard, dirty labor of tannery jobs. They prefer not to use foreign workers, he said, because they are afraid of problems related to drunkenness, violence, and crime.

The second problem is pollution. They originally bought their plant in Yungkang, a sparsely populated rural area near the city of Tainan. As Tainan grew, however, Yungkang quickly developed into a densely populated suburb, and it is no longer feasible for tanneries there to do wet tanning and emit the tanning effluents into the local river. The Lau family solved that problem by moving the wet tanning stage from their Yungkang tannery to China. They bought a tannery in Guangdong, which produces only wet-blue hides. They then import those wet-blue hides into Taiwan and do the dry tanning in Yungkang. When the importing process slows up production, they buy wet-blue hides from other Taiwanese tanneries.

Since this strategy has successfully solved both their labor and environmental control problems, the Laus plan eventually to reduce their Taiwanese operations to only a warehouse and sales operation. "Nowadays, it's too tiring to run a tannery in Taiwan," said Lau Hung-chi. "I think most Taiwanese tanneries will eventually move to China due to Taiwan's labor and environmental problems." Ironically, what he sees as "problems" are actually a manifestation of the improved working conditions and increased desires for ecological sustainability that arose with prosperity and democracy in Taiwan. Moreover, his own perception of racial superiority over "backward" Southeast Asians is the main reason that he does not use foreign labor to solve the labor shortage problem.

THE DIVERSIFIED
STRATEGIES OF PEDRO'S TANNERY

Hok-hing Tannery in rural Jen-te Township of Tainan County faces the same problems, yet I knew it was somewhat different when the thirty-year-old general manager handed me his business card printed in both Spanish and Chinese. Many Taiwanese people select English names for themselves, and most tanners print their business cards in both Chinese and English. This was the first time, however, that I had seen a Taiwanese person use Spanish. He uses the Spanish name Pedro, since he studied Spanish as a student in the foreign language department at National Taiwan University. In his spare time, he still reads Spanish for pleasure. And he relishes the chance to practice his Spanish with Spanish or Latin American leather producers at international leather shows.

Pedro's father was from Tahu in Kaohsiung County, the origin of a whole generation of Taiwanese tanneries. In the early days of the industry, Tahu specialized in tanning. Many of its skilled tanners, including Pedro's father, eventually moved to Tainan to take higher-paying jobs as technicians in such large tanneries as Formosa Leather. He moved to Formosa Leather at the age of sixteen and took a job as a leather splitter. In 1974, he had saved enough money and left Formosa Leather to open up his own tannery. His firm could already afford mechanized splitters but still did much of the work, such as drying, with manual techniques.

The company has stayed in family hands. Pedro, his younger brother, and unmarried younger sister all work in the tannery, in spite of the fact that all three of them have completed university. They often make jokes about their high levels of education, since it is rare for individuals in the industry to have attended university, yet Pedro argues that their higher education levels give them an advantage over other factories. Since he speaks both English and Spanish, he can bypass trading agents and use his foreign language skills to negotiate contracts with shoe factories in Spain, Latin America, and elsewhere. He also says his higher level of education allows him to acquire systematic management techniques that other tanneries are slow to adopt. In the old days, he said, it was sufficient for tanneries to concentrate on learning new technologies, but now the competitive edge comes from acquiring better management skills.

Good management, in fact, has allowed Hok-hing to expand and diversify into other endeavors. In addition to their Tainan leather tannery, they also own a leather waterproofing factory in Yunlin County. That factory does the relatively low-polluting job of gluing polyurethane coating to inner layers of genuine shoe leather. They also run a trading company in Tainan and a pharmaceutical factory and plan to open another tannery in Fujian Province of China next year because, Pedro says, "it's not easy to make leather in Taiwan."

Like other tanneries, Hok-hing faces the two main problems of a labor shortage and increasingly stiff environmental regulations. Pedro solves the labor shortage with a number of different tactics. First, he has hired a team of Thai workers, whom he works until the very early hours of the morning in the busy season. Second, he subcontracts work to smaller tanneries. Subcontracting has the advantages of lightening his own production levels, as well as providing work for companies too weak to develop a stable customer base of their own. Third, he is increasing automation. He has already ordered a fully automatic splitting machine, one of the first in Taiwan.

The second problem is managing environmental pollution. Pedro's tannery has been making leather for twenty-three years. Originally, they were located in Yungkang, but eventually they found it unfeasible to tan leather there as Tainan expanded and neighbors demanded a cleaner environment. Fourteen years ago they moved to a small village in Jen-te Township, where they can still do smelly wet tanning without protests from neighbors. He expects Tainan's urban sprawl to eventually reach Jen-te, which will again create conflict over environmental problems. He thus plans to solve labor and pollution problems by moving production to China. The first to suffer from this move will be the small local subcontractors he employs, as he will be able to take care of all production needs in his Chinese tannery.

Some companies, in fact, have already reduced Taiwanese operations to trade offices and warehouses. One tanner I interviewed owns two large tanneries, employing a total of more than three hundred workers, and a glove factory, with more than five hundred employees, in China. He has never manufactured leather in Taiwan. His office in Tainan County is primarily a trade office and entrepôt, since he buys tanned hides from Taiwanese tanneries to sell to glove and other leather goods factories in China.

These examples, and others like them, show that Taiwan has moved into a new era. Taiwan is no longer an island of living room factories, as it was twenty years ago. Many small firms have now expanded into professionally run corporations. Facing labor and environmental challenges in Taiwan, brought about in part by the growth of labor and environmental movements that demand change, they are now exporting capital and moving production abroad. Since many look directly across the Taiwan Strait, the result is that the economies of Taiwan and China are becoming more closely intertwined than ever before.

CHINESE DREAMS AND TAIWANESE REALITY

The main incentive for Taiwanese manufacturers to move production to China is the relative cost of labor. One tannery worker costs the equivalent of only NT$2,000 a month in China, compared to around NT$30,000 a month in Taiwan. Those labor savings are especially important for labor-intensive industries such as shoe production, but are less important in the relatively capital-intensive tanning industry. Leather tanners emphasize that the purchase of raw hides and chemicals represents their largest capital expenditure and that labor accounts for only a small percentage of their production costs.

Since those imported goods would cost the same or more in China than in Taiwan, total production costs are not significantly lower for them in China. For leather tanners, the main advantage of investment in China is proximity to the labor-intensive leather goods factories producing products such as shoes, belts, and handbags. Since labor is their major expense, these firms have already relocated to China. As the domestic market for tanned leather has diminished rapidly in Taiwan, many tanners consider moving to China to be closer to their major customers. Those who make that move are suddenly confronted with the daily reality of doing business in a different context.

When Taiwanese manufacturers first contemplate moving production to China, they are usually aware of linguistic and cultural similarities. Tanners state that they prefer doing business in China rather than in Thailand or the Philippines because they share a common language with local officials and business partners. In Southeast Asia, inability to communicate in the same language is the major barrier to investment. For the same reason, the Taiwanese have a comparative advantage over Westerners or Japanese when doing business in China. Speaking the same language as their counterparts in China, they can understand each other better and negotiate business deals more easily.

Tanners with experience in China, however, soon begin to perceive important differences. Most importantly, they cite different legal and institutional frameworks in the two places. Since China is well known among tanners for its lenience in regard to pollution control, many tanners contemplate doing wet tanning in China and dry tanning in Taiwan. It is often possible to bypass environmental protection guidelines and even laws by cultivating personal relations with the right people. As one tanner said, "There are many laws," he said, "but China is still a society ruled by men. It's not like Taiwan, a society ruled by law."

Nonetheless, tanners report a number of problems in China. Tanneries rely on large amounts of imported raw materials, including tanning chemicals from Germany, cowhides from North America, and pigskins from Japan. Tanners that stay in Taiwan often cite the relative ease of importing raw materials into Taiwan. Those that invest in China complain about the complex tariffs and bureaucratic hurdles they face when importing raw materials into China. Tanners also complain of the low quality of Chinese domestic pigskins, as China has no standards on slaughtering pigs. Pigs of all ages and sizes are slaughtered together, which reduces the uniformity of the hides produced. In Japan and Taiwan, however, pigs are all slaughtered at a standard weight and size, thus making the hide quality consistent and reliable.

Taiwanese tanners often compare the workforces of Taiwan and China, as if they were comparing different national mentalities. They say that Taiwanese workers have become accustomed to capitalist production and are industrious employees. Due to their Communist past, however, Chinese workers are said to be accustomed to working in state factories with over-inflated workforces and "iron rice bowl" policies that make it impossible to fire them. Taiwanese manufacturers often claim that their workers in China are lazy and require strict supervision in order to meet Taiwanese production standards. Because Chinese factories are not competitive with Taiwanese factories in terms of labor productivity and the quality of the goods produced, customers even feel justified in demanding lower prices for leather tanned in China. These narratives reinforce the perception that Taiwan and China are culturally different from one another.

Tanners investing in China also report excessive regulations and taxes. One tanner, for example, opened up a glove factory in China but has not yet been permitted to repatriate his profits to Taiwan. He said that taxes and tariffs are often raised arbitrarily, and it is often necessary to bribe officials in order to obtain the necessary permits. Fees and taxes imposed by lower-level cadres are often arbitrary and illegal, but he is powerless to stop them. Transportation costs are also much higher in China than they are in Taiwan, because of China's larger size and the inadequacy of the transportation infrastructure. Higher transportation costs cut into their profits and reduce the savings they would otherwise enjoy due to lower labor and land costs.

China is also known for its unstable state policies toward industrial investment. Laws are often unpublished, and changes are made without consultation with the individuals affected. One tannery that has invested in a baseball glove factory in the Philippines said they chose that country over China mainly because state policies in the PRC are too unstable and unpredictable. In a series of case studies drawn from the Fujian press, Thomas Lyons discussed how property rights are threatened by both local village communities and predatory state institutions. In one case, a cement factory was the target of collective violence and was forced to close when villagers would not accept an "outsider" as assistant manager in charge of purchasing and sales (Lyons 1994: 148). Investors, moreover, are only allowed to lease land and cannot purchase it outright. The limited and inconsistent nature of property rights in China is a disincentive to investment in China. The differences between China and Taiwan in all of these areas support perceptions of national difference.

Ironically, the Chinese state is one of the main agents in the creation of a Taiwanese national identity among Taiwanese investors. Since 1987, when Taiwanese visitors and investors were allowed into China, the Chinese state has treated "Taiwan compatriots" *(Taiwan tongbao)* of all ethnic origins in a social category different from Chinese citizens. Like Westerners, Taiwanese business people in China have learned to live with differential treatment in regard to investment terms, rules on property ownership, and even different prices for plane and train tickets. As Melissa Brown noted, "Such treatment runs precisely counter to PRC goals by directly contributing to Taiwanese national identity, for socio-political treatment of people as members of a group promotes those people's identity as a group" (Brown 2004: 240). Taiwanese tanners investing in China resent the fact that China claims Taiwan as its own, yet it treats Taiwanese people as outsiders when they try to do business in China.

Chinese partners are widely perceived as dishonest, and stories abound in Taiwan about investors being cheated in China, even by their own relatives. In some cases, deception has even been institutionalized. One trader, who purchases tanned leather from Shuitou Township in Wenzhou, says traders refer to purchases there as the Shuitou 50 percent cut, since they always get exactly half of the quantity of leather they ordered.

In manufacturing, the stakes are even higher. Because Chinese partners are often dishonest, Taiwanese tanners say they must always ensure that one of their own people is present in the Chinese factory at all times to oversee financial affairs personally. However, this is not always possible. One tannery, for example, eventually backed out of a joint venture in Shandong Province when they discovered that the partners were taking larger profit shares than originally agreed upon. Since they couldn't find a family member willing to go to China, they abandoned the project entirely and now produce all of their leather in Taiwan.

"CULTURAL" DIFFERENCES BETWEEN CHINA AND TAIWAN

Taiwanese investment in China has been bringing the two economies closer together than ever before. Ironically, however, contact between the Taiwanese and the Chinese can also reinforce perceptions that China and Taiwan have become different cultures. Tanners that do business in China often stress the differences between the two places, characterizing the Chinese as greedy, materialistic, and dishonest. The mere fact that they compare China and Taiwan indicates that they perceive them as two different nations and sometimes even as two discrete cultures.

One *thau-ke-niu* with extensive business experience in China asked me if I thought the Chinese and the Taiwanese have the same culture. I said they are very similar, especially the Taiwanese and the Minnan people of Fujian Province. She replied with her own opinion:

The Chinese and the Taiwanese have different national characteristics. Chinese workers are lazy, but Taiwanese workers are used to the idea that they have to work hard if they want to eat. And Chinese are always thinking about money first. When Taiwanese people visit China, their relatives always ask them for money. Older (Taiwanese) people still identify with their hometowns in China and want to go back to visit.[1] But the younger people only identify with Taiwan and don't think they are Chinese.

Skeptical about her claims to unique Chinese and Taiwanese national cultures, I suggested that the Taiwanese are perhaps more honest and less materialistic than their counterparts in China due to different levels of economic development in the two places. Since the Chinese are much poorer, they are often tempted to make easy money from outsiders, and wealthier Taiwanese investors are likely targets for deception. Most Taiwanese, however, are already prosperous. They have no need to cheat others for small amounts of money, and they have the material base that allows them to pursue many other interests other than merely concentrating on earning more money. She, however, insisted that Chinese and Taiwanese people now have completely different cultural values and national identities.

Taiwanese tanners commonly attribute Taiwan's more "modern" culture to the lessons learned during the period of Japanese occupation. One tanner, for example, said that the Japanese taught the Taiwanese honest business practices and general public order, making Taiwan an attractive place to do business. Another tanner, when asked how he thinks Chinese culture influences the leather industry, replied, "I think Japanese culture has influenced management practices more than Chinese culture, because so many Taiwanese companies have their roots in the Japanese occupation of Taiwan." He argued that Taiwan, due to its colonial past, is actually closer to Japan than to China. These sentiments are extremely common among the people I encountered in southern Taiwan. The retelling of these narratives, a daily practice with customers, neighbors, and relatives as well as with visiting anthropologists, contributes to a Taiwanese national identity, not an identity with the People's Republic of China. The constant claims by tanners to identify as modern professionals with links to the Japanese period are best understood in this context.

TAIWAN: A SEAFARING CULTURE?

Taiwanese anthropologist Lin Mei-Rong argues that Taiwan has developed an island culture, which she contrasts to the mainland culture of China. Taiwan is thus more cosmopolitan and open to outside influences than China (Lin 1989: 136). Tanners often told me that exposure to Spanish, Dutch, Japanese, Chinese, and American influences have made the Taiwanese more open to new ideas than the people of most other countries. A Taiwanese "founding myth" is that aboriginal inhabitants of the island were seafarers and had long had trade contacts with other island peoples in the Pacific, notably the Philippines and Japan. The migrants that came to Taiwan were themselves sea traders, fishers and pirates, who were often more at home on the sea than on land. Both the Ming and the Ch'ing states viewed these people with suspicion and tried, albeit with little success, to limit their seafaring ways.

Taiwanese tanners are still as cosmopolitan as their seafaring ancestors. In fact, I found it hard to find tanners for interviews, as they often travel outside of Taiwan. I was often turned away from tanneries on the grounds that the owner was supervising his plant in Guangdong, attending a leather fair in Spain, or merely taking a ski vacation in the Canadian Rockies. The export of capital to China and Southeast Asia is only one manifestation of this tendency. Taiwanese people often emigrate abroad. Most of the wealthy tanning families have already secured their green cards, landed immigrant status, or achieved citizenship in countries such as the United States, Canada, and New Zealand. They sometimes even send family members to Latin America and use those contacts to improve their business profits. Internationalization itself can even create new identities. As one tanner's wife told me: "I am not Chinese, but I am not Taiwanese either. I am a global citizen."

The Tiu family is typical of a wealthy Taiwanese family. They own a large tannery in Pingtung County, and their life is still largely focused on that enterprise. Yet the whole family has already acquired Canadian citizenship, they own a home in Vancouver, and their children are all educated at Canadian universities. The wife's younger sister has moved to Chile with her husband, and they continue to do business with her. They sell the family's tanned leather to leather products companies in Chile, and they also import Chilean canned fish to Taiwan. Ties such as this link Taiwanese people to all parts of the world, diminish their ties to any one nation, and reinforce a cosmopolitan identity far removed from the continental mentality of China.

These people possess important skills, and their human capital has contributed to the development of Taiwan, yet they are highly unlikely to favor unification with China and would probably move elsewhere if the Communists were ever to take over Taiwan. Their investment and emigration strategies, in fact, are calculated to make such a move possible if it were suddenly made necessary. Ironically, it is increased mobility, usually associated with a move from nationalism to globalization, that makes Taiwanese people aware of their nation's marginality. They may perceive themselves as global citizens, but part of globalization includes identification with global practices of citizenship, passports, and nationalism. When they arrive in an international airport or cross a border with a *Republic of China* passport, Taiwanese people often have to explain to confused officials that they are not from the *People's Republic of China* and thus not subject to the strict visa and entry controls placed on citizens of that poorer country. Constantly confronted with this problem, Taiwanese travelers and investors have demanded that their passports be imprinted with the proper name of Taiwan. Globalization thus increases the Taiwanese demand for an independent and internationally recognized nation-state (Wang 2000).

DISCUSSION

Concerned about Taiwan's political future, many tanners brought up the issue of Taiwan's national status. They showed a strong desire to express Taiwanese identity and hoped that I would bring their views into international scholarly discourse. For decades, many Taiwanese people have questioned the nationalist rhetoric of the state, especially because a nationalist ideology was imposed by different groups of outsiders for the second time in recent memory. Now that Taiwan has democratized, the concept of Taiwan as an independent, sovereign state is widely discussed among the population, although many Taiwanese people oppose an outright declaration of independence for fear of a military response from China. Originally, the independence movement was a protest against Nationalist hegemony on the island. Many members of the elder generation perceived the coming of the Kuomintang as a form of external domination, an idea reinforced by the persecution and execution of thousands of Taiwanese in the aftermath of the February 28 incident.

During the course of my fieldwork, I frequently encountered older men who tried to convince me that Taiwan had been colonized by the Chinese Nationalist Party. Some, in fact, refused to speak to me in Mandarin, arguing that it is the language of the colonial oppressor. They encouraged me to learn Taiwanese but spoke to me in Japanese or English to expound on their political ideas. One elderly gentleman spoke to me in Japanese and said that his service in the Japanese military was the proudest moment of his life. These older people represent only the first wave of Taiwanese nationalism, one based on a dichotomy between Native Taiwanese and Mainlanders in Taiwan. For younger generations, however, support for Taiwanese self-determination is motivated more out of satisfaction with their Taiwanese lifestyle and a rejection of potential Communist rule over the island.

The views of the new Taiwanese nationalism are neatly summed up in a discussion I had with one tanner and his wife at the end of our interview. After a discussion of the many problems facing the tanning industry, he said:

Taiwan's biggest problem is the lack of international space. In order to develop further, Taiwan needs recognition as an independent country. Without official recognition as a country, wealth can do nothing for Taiwan. Whenever we go abroad to do business, or just as tourists, we have problems because no one recognizes Taiwan as an independent country.

His wife added:

Taiwan should just do away with the Republic of China and call itself Taiwan. After the Japanese left, we tried to declare the Republic of Taiwan, but then the ROC took over. There were violent conflicts between the Taiwanese and Mainlanders at that time. The Chinese Nationalist Party killed a lot of Taiwanese in the February 28 incident. After that, Mainlanders were afraid to leave their homes, because they were often beaten by Native Taiwanese. But the government repressed the Native Taiwanese movement and oppressed us for many years. If people said the wrong things, they would arrest them and take them away for brainwashing. In school, we were fined one Taiwanese dollar for every sentence of Taiwanese we spoke, since we were expected to learn Mandarin.

Taiwan's national question—to unify with China or take a separate path—seems far out of the range of anthropology. Yet it is important to raise this question precisely because it is one of the most important issues in the lives of Taiwanese people, including the tanners that are the subject of this book. It is also important because it reveals that the cultural arguments of anthropologists often have a political dimension, even if unintended by their authors. Those who study Taiwan as merely an extension of Chinese culture have been criticized for justifying the Chinese Nationalist Party regime (Murray and Hong 1994), and those criticisms deserve consideration. Events after the 1990s—particularly the presidential elections of 2000 and 2004—show just how far the new Taiwanese nationalism has developed since this research was completed. The people of the Chianan Plains, including the tanners of Taiwan, have changed the course of history.

Note

1. Presumably, she was referring to those individuals of recent mainland origin or those who were themselves born in China. As Stevan Harrell pointed out in an early review of this text, few Holo Taiwanese are likely to be any more attached to their "hometowns" in Fujian than Americans would be attached to their ancestral homelands in Africa, Europe, or elsewhere.

CHAPTER NINE

POLITICAL MOVEMENTS— TOWARD A FREE TAIWAN

Today, as a son of a tenant farmer and with a poor family background, I have struggled and grown on this land, and after experiencing defeat and tribulation, I have finally won the trust of the people to take up the great responsibility of leading the country. My individual achievements are minor, but the message is valuable because each citizen of Formosa is a child of Taiwan just like me. The spirit of the "child of Taiwan" reveals to us that even though Taiwan, Penghu, Kinmen and Matsu are tiny islands on the rim of the Pacific, *the map of our dreams knows no limits.*

> —Taiwanese President Chen Shui-bian,
> inauguration address, May 20, 2000
> (emphasis added)

One hot summer day in 2002, I visited one of Tainan County's oldest and wealthiest entrepreneurial families. Unlike most families who prefer living in new concrete homes, the Kho family has proudly maintained their brick and wood home for over a century. The front room, for receiving visitors, was even decorated with a wooden plaque signed by one of the Ch'ing Dynasty emperors to congratulate one of their ancestors for service to China. Yet the glass curio cabinets were filled with Japanese dolls, origami, and antiques. Photos showed the owner posing with Lee Teng-hui, already former president, and Chen Shui-bian, the man from rural Tainan who had been elected president in 2000.

Like many of the leather tanners I had met, my hosts stressed that they had benefited greatly from Japanese education during the colonial period, and they identify as Taiwanese rather than Chinese. They have thus supported the Democratic Progressive Party in Taiwan, with the goal of taking back their land from Mainlander control and protecting it from the possibility of unification with the People's Republic of China. My host said they had already been disenfranchised by the arrival of the Chinese in 1945 and did not wish to endure similar hardship again after having struggled for so long to build up Taiwanese democracy. Taiwan, said the elder Mr. Kho, has been colonized many times and must now stand firm to protect its fragile sovereignty.

After having tea in the formal parlor, the daughter-in-law took me outside to view the grounds of their estate. As we looked out across the verdant fields of rice, she pointed out the irrigation system that had been built by the Japanese during their occupation of Taiwan. Although the concrete embankments and conduits for water seemed to me just part of the landscape, she pointed out that the Chianan Plains irrigation system was among the most advanced in the world at the time and was part of the foundation for Taiwan's subsequent economic growth. Inserting her own family's past into that history, she said:

> All of these fields used to be ours. During the Japanese period, we were a big landlord family. All the peasants in the area worked for us. At harvest time, they brought us rice and left it in this courtyard. We always treated them well as if we were members of one big family. But when the Chinese Nationalist Party came, they implemented land reform, and we lost our land. Those days were over.

This family's history, like those of rural entrepreneurs who built leather tanneries and other manufacturing workshops on land distributed to them during land reform, underscores the fact that Taiwan's "development" experience is much more than an adaptation of Chinese Confucian family patterns to modernity. Development in Taiwan has been a process within which the island's inhabitants have been forced to adapt themselves to institutional frameworks imposed from outside powers including the Manchurian Ch'ing Dynasty, Imperial Japan, and then the Chinese Nationalist Party of Chiang Kai-shek. Each of these colonial regimes was initially foreign to Taiwan and had its own particular class and ethnic struggles to deal with. This book has been about the Chinese Nationalist rule of Taiwan and the beginning phases of decolonization.

After Chiang Kai-shek and the Chinese Nationalist Party arrived in Taiwan in 1945, the Mainlanders from China held the reins of power. In the beginning, they even marginalized the Native Taiwanese from choice jobs with the justification that they did not speak Mandarin well enough. Yet the Chinese

Nationalist Party justified its rule over Taiwan with an ideological claim that Taiwan is essentially a part of Chinese culture. In fact, they often made the claim that Taiwan—as "Free China"—was even more faithful to Chinese culture than the Communist regime in China.

Until martial law was lifted in 1987, few people dared to challenge that ideological hegemony, since proponents of either Chinese communism or Taiwanese independence risked jail sentences or even death. Native Taiwanese who joined the Chinese Nationalist Party even discovered that it worked to their best interest to collaborate and make changes from within the party. That was the strategy of Lee Teng-hui, one that eventually paved the way for important reforms within the party (Lee and Wang 2003; Wachman 1994). By far the most important actors working for democracy, however, were the Taiwanese activists who risked their careers and lives to struggle for change outside of the party.

THE IMPORTANCE OF LABELS

As the critical anthropology of the 1990s has demonstrated, cultural categories are loaded with claims to power. Dirks, Eley, and Ortner wrote, "Cultural (read racial, gender, ethnic, religious) categories provide both a source of oppression and a means for empowering groups and communities to contest that repression" (Dirks, Eley, and Ortner 1994: 24). The denial of Taiwanese self-determination in the name of Chinese culture is an example of this observation. Recognizing the importance of labels, many pro-democracy and human rights advocates have emphasized Taiwanese identity since the early days of Chinese Nationalist rule. For them, assertion of Taiwanese identity is the beginning of empowerment.

This is not to say that Taiwan is unrelated to China. Taiwan clearly has many cultural characteristics in common with China, including kinship patterns, religion, and language. Yet Taiwan also shares many cultural characteristics with Japan and other places. One needs to ask, therefore, why Taiwan is labeled as "Chinese culture," although one would rarely (if ever) describe the United States or Canada primarily as lived variations of "English culture." Naming a culture, including choosing "American culture" or "Canadian culture" over "English culture," is a way of marking the imagined boundaries of nations. It is thus meaningful when Taiwanese people refuse to identify themselves as Chinese. The fact that "Taiwanese culture" is so contentious reveals the power struggle that lies behind national and cultural labels.

The tanners of the Chianan Plains, whose stories make up this ethnography, hold a specific place in the ethnic and class structures of Taiwan. With one exception, they are Native Taiwanese, the inhabitants of Taiwan who were already there when Chiang Kai-shek and the Chinese Nationalist Party arrived in the 1940s. The social structure of the Chianan Plains was radically altered when Chinese forces arrived, oppressed the educated middle class through actions like the February 28 Massacre, and then redistributed land to the tillers in land reform. Many of the tanners were formerly peasants or workers and then became small industrialists with tanneries built on that land. A few were already wealthy people who had profited from collaboration with Japan.

The tanners of Taiwan had been well educated under Japanese rule and were accustomed to industrialization. None of them could speak Mandarin, however, since their lives were conducted in Taiwanese and Japanese. When the Chinese Nationalist forces came to Taiwan, they were suddenly excluded from many employment opportunities on the grounds that they could not speak Mandarin Chinese. There was no better alternative than for them to start small enterprises on the lands given to them in land reform. Those with experience in Japanese tanneries started tanneries of their own, and the Taiwanese tanning industry was born. Since many other industries in Taiwan had the same historical beginning, this is just one example illustrating that the dark side of the "Taiwan miracle" is a saga of military conquest and ethnic domination.

Throughout the rapid industrialization of the 1960s through the 1980s, the tanners and other small manufacturers slowly grew into a new middle class with a power base independent of the Chinese Nationalist Party. What I observed in the 1990s, therefore, was the assertion of a Native Taiwanese middle class in the south of Taiwan. Their evolving national identities were represented in the government with the ascension of President Lee Teng-hui to power and later with the election of Tainan's own Chen Shui-bian as president in 2000 and 2004.

These changes have not taken place without resistance, especially since different regions of Taiwan have different ethnic compositions and thus different nuances in national identity. As one Taipei man once told me, "So-called Taiwan consciousness is really the consciousness of the Chianan Plains." These changes and points of resistance to them are clearly visible during Taiwan's contentious presidential elections. In this concluding chapter, I take a broader look at Taiwan's evolving national identity through the prism of its electoral politics. The elections are the best way to see if the *ethnic* Taiwan consciousness that began in the Chianan Plains has been transformed into a *national* Taiwan consciousness that can unite all regions and ethnic groups on the island.

THE 2000 PRESIDENTIAL ELECTION

During the 2000 presidential campaign, I was doing research in Taipei but making frequent return trips to Tainan. That presidential campaign was marked by division in the ranks of the Chinese Nationalist Party. The Chinese

Nationalist Party ran Lien Chan, vice president under Lee Teng-hui, as its presidential candidate. Born in China to a Taiwanese father, Lien Chan was perceived as Native Taiwanese. He was the favorite candidate of Lee Teng-hui's nativist "mainstream" faction of the party. Mainlander James Soong, who had been named governor by Lee Teng-hui and remained in that post from 1993 to 1998, left the Chinese Nationalist Party and ran on the ticket of his own People First Party. His primary supporters were Mainlanders opposed to party reform, especially any change that would diverge from the goal of eventual unification with China, albeit with the condition that the People's Republic of China evolved into a prosperous and democratic country first. The opposition Democratic Progressive Party ran Tainan's Chen Shui-bian, who had been the defense lawyer for dissidents during the Formosa Incident. His former client, feminist activist Annette Lu, was his vice presidential running mate.

As I traveled between Taipei and Tainan at that time, I found great ambivalence toward Chen Shui-bian and his party, the DPP. Although Chen was widely admired by the Holo Taiwanese of Tainan, there was a perception even in the south that he was anti-business, in the sense of being too favorable toward strict environmental protection and labor regulation. For members of other ethnic groups, moreover, he was perceived as a potentially dangerous proponent of Holo Taiwanese ethnic nationalism. Mainlanders reported being referred to as "Mainland pigs" at DPP rallies and expressed fears that they would become an oppressed majority in the face of ethnic nationalism. They made the argument that a DPP victory would lead to ethnic violence like that which tore apart Yugoslavia. Similar worries were voiced to me by a Hakka interlocutor before the election:

> In the Japanese period, we had to speak Japanese. When the Chinese Nationalist Party came, we had to learn Mandarin Chinese. If the Democratic Progressive Party wins the election, we will all have to learn Taiwanese. It is just another form of hegemony. So we are better with the Chinese Nationalist Party, since everyone speaks Mandarin by now anyway.

After a close race, Chen Shui-bian gained a narrow victory with 39.3 percent of the vote. He was closely followed by James Soong, who gained 36.8 percent, and Lien Chan, who trailed behind with only 23.1 percent. Since the votes of Soong and Lien together added up to nearly 60 percent, it was clear that the election was neither a widespread rejection of the Chinese Nationalist Party nor a clear mandate for Taiwanese nationalism. Domestic dynamics of ethnic composition in voting districts were also very important factors, as they have been for years (Wang 1998).

James Soong won the majority of the votes in most of the country. Mainlander, Hakka, and aboriginal voters tended to support either Lien or Soong, as did many Holo Taiwanese in areas of mixed ethnicity. All of these groups are attracted to the promise of ethnic harmony and frightened by the specter of conflict. Charismatic James Soong, moreover, had cultivated networks of supporters in rural and aboriginal communities during his tenure as governor. In spite of the fact that Soong represented the Mainlander hard-liners in the Chinese Nationalist Party, he would surely have won the election if votes had not been split between him and Lien Chan. That split, however, gave the victory to Chen Shui-bian.

The Holo Taiwanese of the Chianan Plain, that is to say, the tanners of Taiwan and their communities, were the deciding votes. Election results broken down into counties show that the DPP gained most of its support from the Chianan Plains area. The DPP gained its strongest support in 2000 in the southern counties of Changhua, Yunlin, Chiayi, Tainan, Kaohsiung, and Pingtung, as well as Ilan County in the northeast, which is also predominantly Holo Taiwanese. When Chen Shui-bian refers to himself as a "son of Taiwan" rather than as Chinese, the self-proclaimed title is pregnant with meaning.

The significance of his claim, however, depends on who is listening. As his publications and speeches over a career have demonstrated, Chen himself would like to see a united Taiwan, incorporating Native Taiwanese, Mainlanders, and aborigines into his party's vision of civic nationalism. Especially because Chen speaks so often in Taiwanese, and speaks Mandarin with a very heavy Taiwanese accent, his detractors perceive him to be a proponent of the ethnic Holo Taiwanese nationalism supported largely in the south. Chen's challenge for his first term as president, especially if he wished to expand his own power base beyond the Chianan Plain, was to channel latent ethnic Holo nationalism into a civic nationalism embracing all ethnic groups in Taiwan. The success of that project would be tested in the next election.

PRESIDENTIAL CAMPAIGN 2004:
A BATTLE OF IDENTITY

In March 2004, I went to Taiwan as part of a Canadian parliamentary election observer team. This trip gave me a chance to observe the last week of the election campaign, attend official briefings of the main parties, and discuss Taiwanese politics with a variety of people. As Michael Kau at the Ministry of Foreign Affairs summarized events, all nuances in the campaign were related to questions of national identity. What we have been observing in Taiwan, he said, "is a cultural shift as well as a political shift and has long-term political significance." It is thus a story that needs to be told in order to better understand Taiwan.

By 2004, former presidential contenders Lien Chan and James Soong had decided to resolve the differences that split them in 2000 and run together on a joint ticket combining the Chinese Nationalist Party and the People First

Party. This was known as the "pan-blue" team. Since Lien and Soong had won a cumulative vote of 60 percent in the 2000 elections, it was assumed that the pan-blue coalition would easily win. Nonetheless, election polls during the campaign revealed a close race, and the pan-blue candidates had to adopt the tactics of the opposition to retain Holo Taiwanese voters. For example, in spite of coming from the party that once suppressed the Taiwanese language, Lien and Soong both had to campaign in Taiwanese. Although they represented the "pro-unification" party, both Lien and Soong affirmed repeatedly that the Republic of China on Taiwan is an independent and sovereign country. In order to show their love for the soil of Taiwan, they both knelt down and kissed the ground in major media events.

Playing up fears of ethnic Taiwanese nationalism, the Chinese Nationalist Party represented themselves as the only party that could guarantee ethnic harmony. When asked why Taiwanese people should vote for his party, Sun Kwo-hua, a Chinese Nationalist Party member of parliament, said in our briefing, "because we don't want to see a future of division and conflict, whether that be animosity *between our three races* or hostility with China." By three races, he meant the Native Taiwanese, Mainlanders, and aborigines. This discourse, portraying the three groups as essentially different from one another, was a major departure from the pan-Chinese nationalism of the past. He also drew attention to the party's successful development of the Taiwanese economy, and the subsequent economic slowdown from 2000 to 2004 under the DPP, to argue that the Nationalist Party's experience was best for Taiwan's economy.

Just as Soong and Lien had to prove their love for Taiwan, Chen and his "pan-green" coalition had to prove that they represented all Taiwanese ethnic groups and not just Native Taiwanese.[1] In short, the DPP had to negotiate a shift from ethnic to civic nationalism. One element that promised to increase civic nationalism was a highly contested referendum that Chen Shui-bian proposed to hold on the same day as the election. Both referendum questions drew attention away from domestic ethnic conflicts and toward relations with China, and both were actually straightforward questions agreed upon by nearly everyone. The referendum questions read as follows:

Question #1: The people of Taiwan insist that the Taiwan Strait issue be resolved through peaceful means. Should Communist China refuse to withdraw the missiles it has targeted at Taiwan and renounce the use of force against Taiwan, would you agree that the government should acquire more advanced anti-missile systems to strengthen Taiwan's self-defense capabilities?

Question #2: Would you agree that the government should engage in negotiations with Communist China on the establishment of a cross-strait "peace and stability" framework for interaction, in order to build cross-strait consensus and the welfare of people on both sides?

Although Chen Shui-bian insisted that the referendum was not an election strategy, the results would reflect the extent to which the Taiwanese people accepted Taiwanese civic nationalism. Answering yes to the first question would demonstrate a strong consciousness of Taiwan as a nation threatened by the Chinese military. Answering yes to the second question would basically empower Chen to seek formal diplomatic relations with China, affirming the principle of Taiwan and China as sovereign states independent of one another. Even voting no, however, would express an opinion about Taiwan *as a nation* independent of China. The pan-blue coalition was urging a boycott of the referendum, however, and a turnout of less than 50 percent would invalidate the referendum and would suggest that civic nationalism was still not widely accepted. With a focus on civic nationalism, the pan-green coalition used the referendum, as well as slogans of "democratic reform" and "believe in Taiwan," as the most visible component of their electoral campaign.

On the anniversary of the February 28 Massacre, the pan-greens organized a massive rally from the northern to the southern tip of Taiwan. Recalling the ideals espoused in Annette Lu's 1979 speech, the theme was "Ethnic Groups Unite, Holding Hands to Protect Taiwan." More than 2 million people lined the streets and highways of Taiwan, holding hands to show their unity against China. The DPP compared this event to similar demonstrations in the Baltic States that eventually led to independence from the Soviet Union and recognition by the rest of the world. The goal of this rally was to reinforce a sense of national identity with Taiwan and to show the world that Taiwan did not wish to become part of the People's Republic of China.

Many Mainlanders boycotted the February 28 rally, perceiving it to be a manifestation of Native Taiwanese ethnic nationalism that conflated the identities of Communist China, the Chinese Nationalist Party, and by extension the families of those who had come to Taiwan with Chiang Kai-shek. Many even felt frightened that ethnic Taiwanese nationalism would exclude them from the reins of power, just as white South Africans lost influence after the end of apartheid. In response, the pan-blue camp held a series of rallies across Taiwan on March 13, with the themes of "Change the President, Save Taiwan." They portrayed themselves as the only candidates who could guarantee ethnic harmony and economic prosperity. The media, still largely controlled by allies of the Chinese Nationalist Party, claimed that more than 3 million people attended these rallies. On March 10, when the last pre-election polls were published, the media reported that the pan-blue coalition had a slight edge.[2]

A TENSE ELECTION

With large numbers of undecided voters, it was very difficult to predict the outcome of the election. In the end, however, it turned out to be far from a normal election. On the eve of the election, Chen Shui-bian and Annette Lu were campaigning in Chen's hometown of Tainan. As the candidates passed in a jeep through crowds setting off firecrackers, two shots were fired at them. Since Chen was injured in the stomach and Lu in the leg, they were rushed immediately to the hospital. That evening they flew back to Taipei with only minor injuries. Conspiracy theories began to surface, with people in Tainan speculating that the instigators must be either Chinese Communists or pro-unification Mainlander gangs. Some Mainlanders in Taipei suspected that the event had been staged by the DPP in order to generate a sympathy vote for Chen.

Official campaign rallies planned for that evening were immediately cancelled due to fear of ethnic violence, but the election was to go on. On the television news programs, leaders of both parties warned against possible ethnic violence and urged their supporters to stay home. Nonetheless, supporters of both sides still went to the locations where rallies had been planned. Tens of thousands of pan-green supporters crowded around the DPP campaign headquarters in downtown Taipei, waving green flags and singing campaign songs in Taiwanese. Seeing my foreign face, many people approached me with campaign materials, smiles, and excitement for democracy. In front of the campaign headquarters, a group of Buddhist nuns, Protestant ministers, and a Catholic bishop were making a united appeal to support Chen and protect Taiwan's fragile democracy. Each point they made was met with shouts of support and the blowing of horns. In reference to the attempted shootings, one young man walked up to me to say, "The Chinese Nationalist Party has killed many Taiwanese people already. They would surely be able to kill two more in order to regain power." A sense of urgency was in the air, as if this election were Taiwan's last chance for national self-determination.

The pan-blue coalition rally in front of the Chiang Kai-shek Memorial Hall was more subdued. As workers removed the temporary stage and sound system that had been erected for the rally, supporters milled around the square with Nationalist flags and hats showing off the sun symbol of that flag. Vendors stood by tables stocked with campaign paraphernalia, but there were few buyers. Hard-core supporters waved flags and shouted to passing motorists, who honked their horns in reply. The atmosphere there was one of shock and a sense of foreboding. "It's all over," said one supporter sadly. "The shooting will bring out all of the Chen supporters in the south, even the ones who hadn't intended to vote."

That evening, a television talk show was broadcast on several channels with Li Ao, a Mainlander politician who had started Taiwan's only pro-PRC party, the New Party, and Sisy Chen, an independent lawmaker and television commentator, as the main guests. Sisy Chen presented the hypothesis that the shooting had been staged in order to garner sympathy for Chen Shui-bian and influence the elections. They portrayed Chen as a dangerous nationalist demagogue who wanted to create a Republic of Taiwan, even if it meant provoking war with China. When I subsequently talked with people in Tainan on

Figure 9.1   At Chen's 2000 inauguration ceremony, this man walked around holding a sign that read in English, "Taiwan is NOT part of China."

the telephone, they said that anger about the assassination attempt and later accusations on television had mobilized voters even more than the electoral campaign. People embracing all ethnic and national identities felt that this election was the critical last chance to determine their future.

On the morning of March 20, all but one television station started their broadcast with images of Nationalist candidate Lien Chan casting his ballot. The fact that he left the voting station without taking a referendum ballot was strongly emphasized by the commentators. After visiting a voting station at a Taipei school with our delegation, we were able to attend the vote counting at the Central Election Commission. Partisans on both sides watched nervously as a computerized tally showed a very narrow, yet consistent, margin of victory for Chen Shui-bian. Strangely, television stations broadcast results even faster than they were being counted at the Election Commission; flashy graphics showed close results with the candidates alternating in the lead.

By the end of the evening, Chen Shui-bian had indeed won the election. With a voting rate of 80.28 percent, Chen received 50.11 percent of the vote, against 49.89 percent for Lien and Soong. As had happened in the 2000 election, Chen won the majority of the vote in areas dominated by Holo Taiwanese, including a strong showing in the Chianan Plain. Significantly, however, he also had greater support than before in other parts of the country, suggesting that Taiwanese civic nationalism was spreading.

Table 9.1   Voting Patterns by Region, 2004 Presidential Election

District	Chen/Lu		Lien/Soong	
	% of vote in 2004	Relative to 2000 (%)	% of vote in 2004	Relative to 2000 (%)
Taipei City	43.47	+15	56.53	−8
Taipei County	46.94	+35	53.06	−11
Keelung City	40.56	+30	59.44	−14
Taoyuan County	44.68	+50	55.32	−11
Hsinchu City	44.88	+39	55.12	−12
Hsinchu County	35.94	+50	64.06	−8
Miaoli County	39.25	+42	60.75	−18
Nantou County	48.75	+38	51.25	−23
Taichung County	51.79	+44	48.21	−22
Taichung City	47.34	+28	52.66	−16
Hualien County	29.80	+34	70.20	−14
Taitung County	34.48	+43	65.52	−17
Penghu County	49.47	+34	50.53	−20
Lienchang County*	5.76	+220	94.24	−3.6
Kinmen County*	6.05	+95	93.95	−2.5
Changhua County	52.26	+30	47.74	−20
Yunlin County	60.32	+28	39.68	−24
Chiayi County	62.49	+26	37.51	−25
Chiayi City	56.06	+19	43.94	−16
Tainan County	64.79	+20	35.21	−23
Tainan City	57.77	+25	42.23	−21
Kaohsiung County	58.40	+24	41.60	−21
Kaohsiung City	55.65	+22	44.35	−17
Pingtung County	58.11	+26	41.89	−21
Ilan County	57.71	+23	42.29	−20

Source: ROC Central Election Commission

*Lienchang and Kinmen Counties are sparsely populated, heavily militarized islands just off the coast of Fujian Province, China. The extraordinary turnout for the Chinese Nationalist Party is explained by strong military support for the party, as well as local people on the frontlines who fear that the DPP could provoke a war with China.

Table 9.1 shows the results of the 2004 presidential elections. In order to compare the 2000 and 2004 elections, I calculated the percentage difference between the results of the two elections.[3] The regions dominated by Holo Taiwanese are indicated in italics. Chen Shui-bian clearly gained support, whereas Lien and Soong lost voters, in all regions of Taiwan in 2004. Regional disparities related to ethnic composition of voting districts are still evident. Chen Shui-bian won almost exclusively in areas where Holo Taiwanese predominate and where he was strong in 2000. The sole exception was Taichung County, where Soong won in 2000 and Chen won in 2004. These results show that Chen gained support throughout Taiwan but was still very far from achieving a clear national mandate. He would have lost the election, in fact, if it were not for the strong support received from his hometown of Tainan and neighboring counties. In 2004, Chen was still the son of the Chianan Plain rather than the favored candidate of all Taiwan.

Different national imaginations are also reflected in the referendum results. In spite of the electoral victory, the turnout for the referendum disappointed pan-green supporters. The referendum was rendered void because less than 50 percent of eligible voters chose to take part in the referendum. Of the 45 percent who picked up a referendum ballot, 87.37 percent voted yes to the first question on military spending and 84.89 percent voted yes to the second question on pursuing friendly relations with the People's Republic of China.

This referendum failure means that more than half of the eligible voters refused to make a statement on relations between Taiwan and China. This fact shows that civic nationalism in Taiwan was too weak to overcome the pan-blue arguments against the referendum. The strong ethnic nationalism of the Chianan Plain has still not developed into a broader civic nationalism. If anything, a close election following a campaign based on ethnic and national identity only exacerbated the conflicts that have long simmered underneath the surface of Taiwanese social life.

Fallout from the Close Election

After the election results were announced, I immediately telephoned friends in Tainan, who were heartily celebrating Chen's victory. They felt confident that Taiwan was now on the road toward greater democracy and self-determination. I then headed to downtown Taipei with some members of the Canadian delegation to visit both campaign headquarters. The entire district around the DPP campaign headquarters was filled with crowds of joyous supporters. On the edges of the crowd, motorcycles, cars, and taxis sped by, honking their horns and waving green flags out their windows. It was a festive atmosphere with children, grandparents, and even dogs draped in green clothes to show their support for the DPP. On the steps of the campaign headquarters, the crowd was singing, "Taiwan Is My Mother" in Taiwanese. This time, however, the military was also present, setting up a security corridor for the arrival of Chen Shui-bian. They had learned the hard way that Chen's nationalism arouses among some people a dangerous and potentially violent hatred.

Figure 9.2   A disappointed pan-blue supporter at protests after their election defeat.

While a euphoric crowd awaited Chen's victorious arrival at DPP campaign headquarters, sadness and anger filled the air at the Nationalist rally. It was a much smaller crowd. Many of the supporters were already leaving the scene with sad expressions on their faces, limpid flags in their hands. Some were even crying. On the stage, campaign volunteers made speeches urging them not to give up. They said that Chen had only won the election because of a "sympathy vote" after the election and that the election was thus "unfair." With voting results so close, Lien Chan and James Soong refused to concede defeat.

Rumors of ethnic violence once again surfaced. Due to security concerns, we left the rally at the request of the Canadian trade representative in Taipei. When the other members of the delegation returned to the hotel, I went to a Japanese-style hot springs resort in the mountains north of Taipei. Later that evening, I returned to the hotel by taxi. I asked the driver how he felt about the election. "This is the worst disaster that could ever happen," he said. It turns out that he was a sixty-two-year-old Mainlander who had fled from Hankou, China, to Taiwan in 1957 to escape the hunger of the Great Leap Forward. He argued that Chen's Taiwanese nationalism was dangerous, since it encouraged discrimination and even violence against "foreigners" like him.

From his accent, I could tell that he was a Mainlander, but I was surprised to hear him describe himself as a foreigner. "Don't you carry a Republic of China passport?" I asked. "Doesn't that make you Taiwanese?"

"They don't recognize that," he said, referring to the Native Taiwanese. "They think we Mainlanders are not Taiwanese. To them, we are Chinese. We are foreigners."

When we arrived at my hotel, he asked if I had time to talk with him before getting out of the cab. Tears came to his eyes as he discussed the election results, blaming the failure of his party on the people of the Chianan Plain. In a discourse that I would hear later repeated by other Mainlanders, he said:

> The problem is that those people in the south are so uncultured. They were all educated by the Japanese and stopped recognizing that they are Chinese a long time ago. Back then, they thought they were Japanese. Now they think that they are Taiwanese and not Chinese. Sun Yat-sen said that we should make a slow transition from military to tutelary to constitutional rule, but then Lee Teng-hui made the transition to democracy too fast. Now that they have elected Chen Shui-bian, they will even want to establish a Republic of Taiwan. The Republic of China is finished.

Immediately after the election, Lien and Soong promised that they would demand a recount and an investigation of the shooting. In the weeks that followed, tens of thousands of Lien and Soong's supporters protested in Taipei and other cities throughout Taiwan, some even holding a hunger strike in front of the Chiang Kai-shek Memorial. Some of the hard-core Chinese nationalists were angered to see the apparent end of their dream to reunify China under the leadership of the Chinese Nationalist Party. Others were afraid that a DPP majority would turn Mainlanders into a despised ethnic minority, or even "push the Mainlanders into the sea."

Native Taiwanese were also frightened. Rumors on the Internet suggested that Mainlander gang members dressed like DPP supporters were planning on attacking elderly Mainlander veterans at the anti-Chen protests to spark ethnic violence. The specter of ethnic conflict between Mainlanders and Native Taiwanese seemed so close that religious leaders, women's groups, and aboriginal elders all made public calls for reconciliation. The protesters, however, eventually dispersed and life returned to normal.

In the aftermath of these events, both parties seriously reflected on how they could improve their own positions in terms of ethnic and national identity. Having been accused of fomenting ethnic division to win the election, the victorious Chen Shui-bian promised to hold an ethnic and cultural development conference to ameliorate ethnic relations. In a forum with university students, Chen said, "The ethnic issue concerns not just the identification of the country but also perspectives on cultural differences and language. Therefore, we must call a national conference to discuss the ethnic and cultural developments in our country" (Huang and Lin 2004). The conference, bringing together anthropologists, other scholars, and policymakers, was held in October 2004.

The Chinese Nationalist Party was also forced to reflect on the reasons for their defeat in a time of increased national identification with Taiwan. On April 7, Central Standing Committee member Hung Yu-chin even suggested that the party be renamed the Taiwan Nationalist Party to keep up with new trends. Although no formal resolution was made, the suggestion received support, especially from members who represent southern constituencies. Former Kaohsiung mayor Wu Duen-yih said, "When you say 'Chinese,' it is the people's general impression that it refers to the other side of the Strait. By doing away with the word 'Chinese,' we can save the party many unnecessary attacks from political opponents" (Huang 2004). Chinese identity, once the cornerstone of Nationalist hegemony on Taiwan, has begun to lose its sacred stature, even in some factions of Chiang Kai-shek's old party.

CONCLUSIONS

Taiwan's debates about ethnic and national "Chineseness" have important lessons for anthropology. Most of all, they teach us that ethnic and national labels are problematic. Trained in a long tradition of cultural relativism, from its roots in the thought of Max Weber to contemporary disciples of Clifford Geertz, many anthropologists have learned to label national or ethnic groups and then to explain the behavior of their members as motivated by "culture." By doing so, they have overlooked the political and often nationalistic processes that created those cultural categories in the first place. Their works have masked power struggles based on other forms of identity and thus contributed to the legitimatization of regimes of power such as the Chinese Nationalist Party in Taiwan. Through their assertions that the Taiwanese are not Chinese, the tanners of Taiwan made me see that my own cultural categories reflected political power.

The discourse asserting that the Taiwanese people represent Chinese culture and that the "Taiwanese miracle" would have been impossible without that heritage is the main storyline in a development narrative that justified Chinese Nationalist rule over Taiwan. In the anthropology of Taiwan, an emphasis on kinship and religion made it appear that the predominance of small firms in Taiwan's development is largely a product of Chinese family culture. This discourse of Taiwan as traditional China was of course the product of a specific conjuncture in global political economy. It permeated anthropology during the Cold War at precisely the time when a Chinese alternative was needed to the Communist mainland.

These cultural approaches led many anthropologists and some development specialists to skim lightly over other influences on Taiwan's development, including the legacy of Japanese colonialism, the land reform that gave the means of production to families, and a repressive political environment that led most Native Taiwanese to focus their energies on entrepreneurship rather than politics. It also overlooked the diversity that characterized the industrial structure of the country. The tanners of Taiwan made this clear to me by challenging my views on "Chinese culture" and by educating me about such topics as the February 28 Massacre. Their narratives are a form of resistance and demonstrate the existence of a Taiwanese national identity.

When I moved to Tainan to study the relationship between Chinese culture and development in the leather industry, some tanners encouraged me to focus instead on Taiwanese history and the colonial situation under the Chinese Nationalist Party. Others resisted cultural explanations by strongly emphasizing that their firm organization and business practices are the rational choices of modern entrepreneurs. Their decisions to present themselves to me in terms of professional rather than cultural identity are important. Knowing that I would eventually publish a book about Taiwan, these tanners wanted to present Taiwan as a modern country that has evolved from its Chinese roots.

Of course, the conflict between ethnic groups and their respective national identities is not the only power struggle in Taiwan. An exclusive focus on that would represent only the perspective of the bosses. Within the workplaces of southern Taiwan, there are other power struggles based on gender and class. In this book, I have shown how boss-wives, long perceived as subordinate to their husbands, assert power in the workplace by taking control of important management tasks. I have also demonstrated how class identity has been subdued through a range of strategies. The most important strategy in recent years has been the importation of foreign workers, which divides the working class according to nationality. These two groups of workers can barely communicate with each other, let alone organize resistance.

These gender and ethnic struggles are also related to national identity, but not reducible to it. The narrative of women's emancipation from Confucianism carries nationalist connotations, since it evokes the image of evolution away from Chinese culture and toward modernist ideals of gender equality. The choice of a woman as vice president reinforces that image. Sometimes, however, women's power is explicitly linked to a primordial Taiwanese identity. One interlocutor, cited at the beginning of Chapter 6, even argued that Taiwanese women were always strong until they were oppressed by Japan and China. Related to this claim are ideas that aboriginal women are more powerful than Chinese women and that aboriginal women are the maternal ancestors of the Taiwanese. These tropes are common in the narratives of southern Taiwanese. Women's emancipation has thus become tied to national imaginations.

The interplay between class and national identity is also important. At one level, bosses stress cultural norms labeled as Taiwanese to argue against the introduction of labor unions in their factories. They also use a mix of Taiwanese and foreign workers to keep wages low, ensure a docile workforce when overtime work is needed, and prevent unified opposition. Foreign workers are depicted as prone to violence and drinking, yet more capable of working overtime than Taiwanese workers. Especially with the presence of foreign workers, Taiwanese workers perceive national identity to be more important than class identity.

With the rapid expansion of trade relations between China and Taiwan in the 1990s, Taiwanese investors in China finally had the opportunity to experience life and work in China firsthand. In the leather industry, some tanners have moved production to China to be closer to the downstream industries that manufacture shoes and other leather products. To a certain extent, their experiences have also contributed to a Taiwanese identity, since they find that business ethics, work ethics, and legal norms differ greatly between the two countries. Taiwanese investors are even treated as outsiders in China, which increases their subjective feelings of difference. This suggests that increased contact between China and Taiwan actually contributes to a stronger Taiwanese national identity, at least among southern Taiwanese entrepreneurs.

All of this has happened in the context of political change following the lifting of martial law in 1987. During the presidencies of Lee Teng-hui and Chen Shui-bian, public discourse began to shift from hegemonic Chinese nationalism to a fiercely contested battle between Chinese consciousness and Taiwanese consciousness. That battle is far from over. As Ernest Gellner pointed out, "Nationalism is not the awakening of nations to self-consciousness; it invents nations where they do not exist" (Anderson 1991: 6). What I observed in Taiwan over the past decade was the end of Chinese Nationalist Party hegemony and the invention of new national imaginings. The struggle over who will invent the national community of Taiwan is still in its early stages.

The ruling DPP has a difficult project of national construction ahead of them, and culture will be a central part of that. The challenge is to construct a new Taiwanese national culture that is not reducible to the ethnic nationalism of the Holo Taiwanese. The extent to which Taiwanese nationalism is identified with that one group will determine the level of support of Mainlanders, Hakka, and aboriginal people for opposition parties promising ethnic harmony. It even makes many Native Taiwanese perceive the DPP as troublemakers. At the same time, however, the familiar Chinese cultural nationalism hardly serves their purpose either, as it frames unification with the People's Republic of China as a logical possibility. This is no longer a popular option in Taiwan.

Taiwan is thus setting off into unknown territory. It is impossible to predict the fate of this young nation or even whether it will survive its very difficult challenges as it struggles for international recognition. Most importantly, the People's Republic of China has not yet renounced the threat of force if Taiwan does not eventually surrender its sovereignty and become a Chinese province.

Amidst these changes, Taiwan is an exciting place to conduct anthropological research precisely because it allows one to observe a new nation and a new culture evolving in present time. Taiwan demonstrates well that culture is not unitary and bounded, nor is it explanatory of anything. Instead, it is the product of political and economic forces, constantly being dismantled and reconstructed according to the needs of the moment. Chen Shui-bian underlined the constructed nature of nations in his 2000 inauguration speech when he referred to "the map of our dreams." Maps have long marked off national imaginations, and cultures have often been used to color in the spaces. Anthropology is just another tool in the ideological toolkit if it is used to justify blue, green, or any other color on the map. An empowering anthropology, however, must reveal the power struggles that motivate and inform the cartographers.

Notes

1. The pan-green coalition also included the Taiwan Solidarity Union, a small pro-DPP splinter group that left the Chinese Nationalist Party with Lee Teng-hui.

2. In Taiwan, electoral laws forbid the publication of poll results within ten days of an election, since manipulation of poll results could influence voter behavior.

3. In 2000, Lien and Soong ran on separate ballots. I added their separate election results before calculating the relative change in support between the two elections.

Appendix I: Glossary

Austronesian—A language family found throughout the Pacific. The Austronesian speakers of Taiwan constitute the island's indigenous population.

Chen Shui-bian (b. 1951)—President of Taiwan from 2000 to the present.

Chianan Plain—The fertile plains of southwestern Taiwan, extending from Changhua County to Kaohsiung County.

Chiang Ching-kuo (1909–1988)—Son of Chiang Kai-shek. After inheriting the presidency from his father, he ruled Taiwan until his death in 1988.

Chiang Kai-shek (1888–1975)—Military and political leader of the Chinese Nationalist Party who ruled over Taiwan from 1945 until his death in 1975.

Chinese Nationalist Party, or Kuomintang (KMT)—A political party established in China by Sun Yat-sen in 1912. Their party-state apparatus controlled Taiwan from 1945 until democratization and their first electoral defeat in 2000.

Ch'ing Dynasty—The imperial government of China from 1644 to 1911, which gradually increased its rule over Taiwan from 1683 to 1895, when China ceded the island to Japan.

class-for-itself—In Marxist terminology, the subjective class identity that leads to political mobilization and class struggle.

class-in-itself—In Marxist terminology, the objective existence of different positions in the mode of production.

Confucianism—A system of ethics based on the writings of the Chinese philosopher Confucius (551–479 B.C.E.). Confucianism was emphasized as part of the nationalist ideology of the Chinese Nationalist Party in Taiwan.

cuxin—In Mandarin, coarseness or carelessness, often seen as a masculine characteristic.

Democratic Progressive Party (DPP)—The opposition party founded in Taiwan in 1986, which has held the presidency in Taiwan since 2000.

149

February 28 Massacre—On February 28, 1947, two years after Chiang Kai-shek's
Chinese Nationalist Party had taken over Taiwan, Chiang's military massacred
a still unknown number of civilians, after Native Taiwanese launched a social
movement demanding democratic reform.

Formosa Incident—The suppression of a demonstration in Kaohsiung in 1979, which
inspired a generation of pro-democracy activism.

geomancy—The art of manipulating natural energies of the landscape to influence
human destiny.

goa-hang—"Insiders" to an occupation, or specialists.

Hakka—An ethnic group in Taiwan whose ancestors came to the island from Guangdong Province of China from the seventeenth to nineteenth centuries.

hegemony—Power exercised in society through ideological means rather than
through brute force.

Holo—An ethnic group in Taiwan whose ancestors came to the island from Fujian
Province of China from the seventeenth to the nineteenth centuries.

kam-cheng—A concept referring to emotional bonds between people, often used in
negotiating relations between people.

Koxinga—The Chinese rebel who ruled Taiwan from 1661 to 1683 in the name of the
Ming Dynasty.

jin-cheng-bi—Friendliness or hospitality, the "human touch" that Taiwanese say they
bring to everyday transactions.

lai-hang—"Outsiders" to an occupation, or nonspecialists.

land reform (1951)—The land-to-the-tiller reform carried out in Taiwan by the
Chinese Nationalist Party to break the island's ruling class and increase their
support among the peasantry.

Lee Teng-hui (b. 1923)—Native Taiwanese politician who succeeded Chiang Kai-shek
to the presidency in 1988 and was re-elected in the first direct presidential elections in 1996.

Lien Chan (b. 1936)—Vice president under Lee Teng-hui and unsuccessful candidate
for president on the Chinese Nationalist Party ticket in both 2000 and 2004.

Lu, Annette (Lu Hsiu-lien) (b. 1944)—Feminist and human rights activist who served
as vice president of Taiwan beginning in 2000.

Mainlanders—An ethnic group in Taiwan composed of the Chinese who came to the
island with the Chinese Nationalist Party beginning in 1945.

Mandarin Chinese—The official language of China, based on the Beijing dialect,
which has been imposed on the population of Taiwan by the Chinese Nationalist Party.

matrilocality—The practice of living with the bride's family after marriage.

Native Taiwanese—Referring usually to the Hakka and Holo, the ethnic groups already present in Taiwan before 1945, when the island was taken over by the
Chinese Nationalist Party.

nuqiangren—"Strong women," an appellation for women successful in business or
other careers.

obaasan—The Japanese word for "grandmother," used in Taiwan in reference to elderly women.

patrilineality—The practice of transmitting property through the male line.

patrilocality—The practice of living with the groom's family after marriage.

People First Party—A pro-unification party established by James Soong in reaction to perceived indigenization of the Chinese Nationalist Party.

People's Republic of China—The state established in China by the Chinese Communist Party in 1949.

Republic of China—The Chinese government established in 1912. Its area of effective jurisdiction was reduced to Taiwan after the Communists gained control of China in 1949.

sinicization—The process of adopting characteristics perceived as Chinese, comparable to westernization.

Soong, James (Soong Chu-yu) (b. 1942)—Taiwanese politician and unsuccessful candidate for president in 2000 and for vice president in 2004.

Sun Yat-sen (1866–1925)—The "father of the Chinese nation" and founder of the Chinese Nationalist Party.

Taiwanese language—The native language spoken by the Holo ethnic group of Taiwan.

thau-ke—The Taiwanese term for "boss."

thau-ke-niu—The Taiwanese term for "boss-wife."

Three Principles of the People—Nationalism, democracy, and people's livelihood: the basis of the Nationalist Party ideology formulated by Sun Yat-sen and promulgated in Taiwan by the Chinese Nationalist Party.

tong-hang—Members of the same occupation.

Treaty of Shimonoseki (1895)—The treaty in which China ceded Taiwan to Japan after defeat in the Sino-Japanese War.

White Terror—The forty years of martial law in Taiwan from 1947 to 1987, during which time the state oppressed people suspected of supporting either communism or Taiwanese independence.

xixin—In Mandarin, meticulousness or attention to detail, often seen as a feminine characteristic.

Appendix II:
The Labor Process of
Leather Tanning

L eather tanning is the process that transforms the delicate hides of dead animals, which would otherwise quickly decay and rot, into sheets of sturdy leather that can be used to make a wide variety of products such as shoes, luggage, or furniture upholstery. It is basically a recycling process, transforming the by-products of the meat industry into useful consumer goods. Taiwanese tanneries use some fresh hides, mostly pigskins, from domestic slaughterhouses. Since the Taiwanese eat pigskins, however, and the island's cattle population is limited, both pigskins and cowhides are imported. Imported hides are salt-pickled in the country of origin in order to prevent the fragile hides from decomposing during transport.

Tanners described the tanning process as a complex art, and they take pride in mastering the difficult skills needed to make high-quality leather. One second-generation tanner I interviewed said he originally planned another career in electronics but eventually took over his father's tannery after he discovered the challenges of tanning and the satisfaction that could be gained from mastering it:

> After military service, I came back to my father's tannery. I studied electronics part-time and worked in the tannery part-time. It was then that I became interested in leather tanning. Leather goes through a lot of changes, so it's difficult to research it. First of all, there are many different kinds of skins, each kind presenting its own problems. Hides differ depending on whether the cow is large or small, male or

female, depending on the climate and on the different breeds of cow. They can even differ depending on the time of year they are killed. Cows have short hair in the summer and long hair in the winter. The skins of Canadian cows are very thick because the climate there is so cold. Canadian cows make the best leather. The skins of Texan cows are very thin because the climate there is so hot. We can't just tan all of these skins in the same way. We have to adjust for these differences in the tanning process, using different quantities of chemicals and tanning the hides for longer or shorter periods of time. I find leather tanning interesting because it gives me a feeling of success.

The process of tanning is divided into stages of wet and dry tanning. Wet tanning is considered to be the most difficult and dangerous stage of leather tanning, and it is the most polluting. In the early days, tanning was done in pits by submerging the hides in a solution of water and the tannic acid from tree bark, a process from which the English word tanning is derived. All Taiwanese tanneries now use modern chrome tanning methods, in which hides are placed in large, mechanical tanning drums. The drums rotate automatically, ensuring that the hides are evenly treated with a solution of water and chrome-based chemicals.

The process of removing the hides from these drums is the most unpleasant task in the tanning business. The drums open up, spurting pools of blue water and hides onto the factory floor. The workers, equipped with tall rubber boots, wade into the solution and drag out the wet hides. In the process, they become covered in water, salt, fat, and blood from the hides, as well as with chemical residue. This work requires great strength, as wet cowhides can weigh up to 50 kilograms.

The Taiwan Regional Association of Tanneries divides the wet tanning process into the following eleven steps. Steps one through six are preparatory steps and are often done at the slaughterhouse or by foreign hide agents before export to Taiwan.

Wet Tanning

1. *Trimming and sorting.* This preparatory step is done in the receiving warehouse when hides and skins are delivered to the tannery. This step was important in the early days of tanning, when tanners still relied on local slaughterhouses for hide supplies. Certain parts of the body, such as the head and hooves, are useless to tanners and can actually harm their equipment if processed with the hides. These parts must be cut off and discarded.

2. *Soaking.* The first stage of tanning is soaking the hides in a wetting solution and antibacterial agents in large tanning drums. Fresh hides must be soaked in order to remove any blood or other liquids that may have remained in the hides. Preserved hides must be soaked in order to restore the water to the hides that had been removed during the salting process. This stage also rinses away salt and other pollutants. Hides are soaked for a period of eight to twenty-four hours, depending on their thickness.

3. *Fleshing.* The underside of the skins and hides often retains some excess meat and fat. These are removed from the skins with fleshing machines before the hides are

processed. In the old days, poorer families would cut off the meat scraps by hand and use them to make soup. Nowadays, some tanneries still find a use for these scraps, selling them for use as fertilizer.

4. *De-hairing.* This step removes excess hair, epidermis, and soluble proteins from the upper side of the skins or hides. Chemical agents, usually based on lime, remove the hair while retaining the collagen needed during tanning.

5. *De-liming.* In this step, the hides are rinsed in clear water in order to remove the lime that was used in the de-hairing process. Enzymes are used to remove hair roots, pigments, and other parts of the skin not needed in leather. The quantities of chemicals used in this stage, as well as the time needed to complete the process, vary according to the quality of the skins and the pH level of the local water supply. Technicians thus need a great deal of experience to consistently produce leather of good quality.

6. *Pickling.* This is the final preparatory stage before tanning can commence. Since chrome tanning agents cannot dissolve and enter the hides at a high pH level, sulfuric acid is added to lower the pH level and increase the acidity of the hides. The hides are first salted in order to strengthen the fibers of the hides and prevent acidic swelling, which can lessen the quality of the leather produced. While the hides are still in the tanning drums, salt is added and then sulfuric acid.

7. *Tanning.* Tanning is the stage that transforms fragile hides into stable leather that can resist rot and decay. It is a chrome-based chemical process that strengthens the collagen in the hides. Tanning is done in large rotating drums, a process that takes about four to six hours, depending on the thickness of the hides. Care must be taken that the protein fibers are evenly tanned. The water temperature and amount of chemicals used can influence the quality of the leather, and adjustments must be made for differences in the raw hides and skins themselves. At the end of the tanning process, hides take on a bluish green color and are called wet-blue hides.

8. *Wringing.* After tanning, the hides are put through a wringing machine to press out the water they have absorbed during the previous steps.

9. *Splitting and shaving.* Due to differences in climate or the age of the animals slaughtered, the thickness of animal hides differs greatly, yet tanneries must produce leather of standard thickness to meet the specifications of their customers. Furthermore, the different layers are used to produce different kinds of leather. Leather can be split into three layers: upper leather from the outer surface of the skins, lining leather from the second layer, and split leather, used to make suede, from the inner layer of the skins. Splitting machines can now split leather to a precision of one-hundredth of an inch.

10. *Retanning, coloring, fat liquoring.* These steps change the quality of the leather to meet manufacturers' specifications. Retanning is done to give the finished leather the qualities of leather produced with different tanning agents. Natural tanning agents such as acids derived from oak, silk wood, hemlock, or quebracho are used in this stage. Finished leather varies in texture and solidity according to the tanning agent used in retanning. Coloring uses a variety of different dying agents to produce leather of different colors. Fat liquoring uses vegetable or mineral oil to lubricate the leather fibers and make adjustments in the texture of the finished product.

11. Setting out. In this stage, the leather is stretched out and pressed in large stretching machines. This step reduces the water quantity in the leather to about 60 percent.

Dry Tanning

1. Drying. In the early days of tanning, the hides were nailed to boards and set out in the sun to dry. Today tanneries now usually use vacuum drying machines to bring the tanned leathers to equilibrium moisture.

2. Conditioning. After drying, the leather becomes too hard to be used in some consumer products, like sport shoes or gloves. In the conditioning stage, a controlled amount of water is put back into the leather, which is then coated with water resistant chemicals to retain the moisture.

3. Staking. This is the final stage of softening leather. The sheets of leather are put through a staking machine that manipulates the fibers to produce the required degree of softness.

4. Buffing. Natural leather often has parasitic damage or scratches on the hide, which is still visible after tanning. Since natural grain is the best proof that the leather is genuine, this stage is sometimes skipped entirely. Unbuffed leather is called full grain leather, and the grain is still visible. Buffing, on the other hand, produces smooth, finished leather with a standard appearance.

5. Finishing. This stage gives the leather its final appearance. A chemical coating is added to protect the leather from damage or stains. In this stage, the leather may be dyed different colors and treated to have a glossy or matte appearance.

6. Measuring. In this stage, the surface area of the leather is measured, and the price is set. This is done quickly and easily by passing the sheets of leather under a computer scanner.

7. Grading. In this final stage before shipping, the leather is graded according to texture, uniformity of color, thickness, and surface defects.

References

Adrian, Bonnie. 2003. *Framing the Bride: Globalizing Beauty and Romance in Taiwan's Bridal Industry*. Berkeley: University of California Press.

Anderson, Benedict. 1991. *Imagined Communities: Reflections on the Origin and Spread of Nationalism*. London: Verso Press.

Appadurai, Arjun. 1996. *Modernity at Large: Cultural Dimensions of Globalization*. Minneapolis: University of Minnesota Press.

Arrigo, Linda Gail. 1985. "Economic and Political Control of Women Workers in Multinational Electronics Factories in Taiwan: Martial Law Coercion and World Market Uncertainty." *Contemporary Marxism* (11): 77–95.

———. 1998. "Fifty Years After 2-2-8: The Lingering Legacy of State Terror in the Consolidation of Bourgeois Democracy in Taiwan." *Humboldt Journal of Social Relations* (23): 47–69.

Barrett, Richard. 1988. "Autonomy and Diversity in the American State on Taiwan." In *Contending Approaches to the Political Economy of Taiwan*, edited by E. Winckler and S. Greenhalgh, pp. 121–137. Armonk, N.Y.: M. E. Sharpe.

Barth, Fredrik, ed. 1969. *Ethnic Groups and Boundaries: The Social Organization of Culture Difference*. Boston: Little and Brown.

Bhabha, Homi K., ed. 1990. *Nation and Narration*. London: Routledge.

Blim, Michael. 1990. *Made in Italy: Small-Scale Industrialization and Its Consequences*. New York: Praeger.

Brown, Melissa. 1996. *Negotiating Ethnicities in China and Taiwan*. Berkeley: Institute of East Asian Studies.

———. 2004. *Is Taiwan Chinese? The Impact of Culture, Power, and Migration on Changing Identities*. Stanford: Stanford University Press.

Burawoy, Michael. 1979. *Manufacturing Consent*. Chicago: University of Chicago Press.

———. 1985. *The Politics of Production*. London: Verso.

Chang, Mau-kuei. 2003. "On the Origins and Transformation of Taiwanese National Identity." In *Religion and the Formation of Taiwanese Identities,* edited by P. R. Katz and M. A. Rubinstein, pp. 23–58. New York: Palgrave Macmillan.

Chatterjee, Partha. 1993. *The Nation and Its Fragments: Colonial and Postcolonial Histories.* Princeton: Princeton University Press.

Chen, Lung-chu, and W. M. Reisman. 1972. "Who Owns Taiwan: A Search for International Title." *Yale Law Journal* 81 (4): 599–671.

Chung, Chi-nien. 2004. "Institutional Transition and Cultural Inheritance: Network Ownership and Corporate Control of Business Groups in Taiwan, 1970s–1990s." *International Sociology* 19 (1): 25–50.

Cohen, Myron. 1976. *House United, House Divided: The Chinese Family in Taiwan.* New York: Columbia University Press.

Comaroff, John, and Jean Comaroff. 1992. *Ethnography and the Historical Imagination.* Boulder: Westview Press.

Corcuff, Stephane, ed. 2002a. *Memories of the Future: National Identity Issues and the Search for a New Taiwan.* Armonk, N.Y.: M. E. Sharpe.

———. 2002b. "The Symbolic Dimension of Democratization and the Transition of National Identity under Lee Teng-hui." In *Memories of the Future: National Identity Issues and the Search for a New Taiwan,* edited by S. Corcuff, pp. 73–101. Armonk, N.Y.: M. E. Sharpe.

de Glopper, Donald. 1978. "Doing Business in Lukang." In *Studies in Chinese Society,* edited by A. Wolf, pp. 291–320. Stanford: Stanford University Press.

DGBAS (Directorate-General of Budget Accounting and Statistics). 1993. *The Report on the 1991 Industrial and Commercial Census, Taiwan-Fukien Area, ROC.* Vol. 3, *Manufacturing.* Taipei: Executive Yuan.

Dirks, Nicolas B., Geoff Eley, and Sherry B. Ortner, eds. 1994. *Culture/Power/History: A Reader in Contemporary Social Theory.* Princeton: Princeton University Press.

Dirlik, Arif. 1997. "Critical Reflections on 'Chinese Capitalism' as Paradigm." *Identities* 3 (3): 303–330.

Edmondson, Robert. 2002. "The February 28 Incident and National Identity." In *Memories of the Future: National Identity Issues and the Search for a New Taiwan,* edited by S. Corcuff, pp. 25–46. Armonk, N.Y.: M. E. Sharpe.

Embree, Bernard L. M. 1984. *A Dictionary of Southern Min.* Taipei: Taipei Language Institute.

Executive Yuan. 1954. *Statistics of Manufacturing Industry,* Vol. 6. Taipei: Executive Yuan.

Executive Yuan Council of Labor Affairs. 1995. *Yearbook of Labor Statistics.* Taipei: Executive Yuan.

———. 2003. *Yearbook of Labor Statistics.* Taipei: Executive Yuan.

Feld, Steven, and Keith H. Basso. 1996. *Senses of Place.* Sante Fe: School of American Research Press.

Fried, Morton. 1969 [1953]. *The Fabric of Chinese Society: A Study of Social Life in a Chinese County Seat.* New York: Octagon Books.

Gallin, Bernard, and Rita Gallin. 1982. "Socioeconomic Life in Rural Taiwan: Twenty Years of Development and Change." *Modern China* 8 (2): 205–246.

Gates, Hill. 1981. "Ethnicity and Social Class." In *The Anthropology of Taiwanese Society,* edited by E. A. Martin and H. Gates, pp. 241–281. Stanford: Stanford University Press.

_____. 1996a. *China's Motor: A Thousand Years of Petty Capitalism.* Ithaca: Cornell University Press.

_____. 1996b. "Owner, Worker, Mother, Wife: Taibei and Chengdu Family Businesswomen." In *Putting Class in Its Place,* edited by Elizabeth Perry, pp. 127–165. Berkeley: Institute of East Asian Studies.

Gold, Thomas. 1986. *State and Society in the Taiwan Miracle.* Armonk, N.Y.: M. E. Sharpe.

Goody, Jack. 1990. *The Oriental, the Ancient, and the Primitive: Systems of Marriage and the Family in the Pre-industrial Societies of Eurasia.* Cambridge: Cambridge University Press.

Government Information Office. 1997. *ROC Yearbook.* Taipei: Kwang Hwa Publishers.

Gramsci, Antonio. 1971. *Selections from the Prison Notebooks.* Edited by Quintin Hoare and Geoffrey Nowell Smith. London: Lawrence and Wishart.

Greenhalgh, Susan. 1984. "Networks and Their Modes: Urban Society on Taiwan." *China Quarterly* 99: 529–552.

_____. 1988. "Families and Networks in Taiwan's Economic Development." In *Contending Approaches to the Political Economy of Taiwan,* edited by E. Winckler and S. Greenhalgh, pp. 224–245. Armonk, N.Y.: M. E. Sharpe.

_____. 1994. "De-orientalizing the Chinese Family Firm." *American Ethnologist* 21 (4): 746–775.

Gupta, Akhil, and James Ferguson. 1997. *Culture, Power, Place: Explorations in Cultural Anthropology.* Durham, N.C.: Duke University Press.

Harrell, Stevan. 1982. *Ploughshare Village: Culture and Context in Taiwan.* Seattle: University of Washington Press.

_____. 1985. "Why Do the Chinese Work So Hard? Reflections on an Entrepreneurial Ethic." *Modern China* 11: 203–226.

Hobsbawm, Eric, and Terence Ranger, eds. 1983. *The Invention of Tradition.* Cambridge: Cambridge University Press.

Hsiao, Michael Hsin-Huang. 1990. "Emerging Social Movements and the Rise of a Demanding Civil Society in Taiwan." *Australian Journal of Chinese Affairs* (24): 163–179.

Hsiung, Ping-Chun. 1996. *Living Rooms as Factories: Class, Gender, and the Satellite Factory System in Taiwan.* Philadelphia: Temple University Press.

Huang, Hua. 1995. "Leather Industry." In *1994 Industrial Development Yearbook of the Republic of China,* pp. 531–535. Taipei: Ministry of Economic Affairs Industrial Development Bureau.

Huang, Jewel, and Chieh-yu Lin. "Chen Vows to Tackle Ethnic Conflict," *Taipei Times,* April 13, 2004, http://www.taipeitimes.com/News/front/archives/2004/04/13/2003136555, (last accessed November 8, 2004).

Huang, Tai-lin. "Top KMT Figure Plays Name Game." *Taipei Times,* April 8, 2004, http://www.taipeitimes.com/News/front/archives/2004/04/08/2003135791 (last accessed November 8, 2004).

International Committee for Human Rights in Taiwan. 1981. *The Kaohsiung Tapes*. Seattle: International Committee for Human Rights in Taiwan, http://www.taiwandc.org/kao-tapes.pdf (last accessed November 8, 2004).

Ka, Chih-ming. 1995. *Japanese Colonialism in Taiwan: Land Tenure, Development, and Dependency, 1895–1945*. Boulder: Westview Press.

Katz, Paul. 2003. "Identity Politics and the Study of Popular Religion in Postwar Taiwan." In Religion and the Formation of Taiwanese Identities, edited by P. R. Katz and M. A. Rubinstein, pp. 157–180. New York: Palgrave Macmillan.

Katz, Paul R., and Murray A. Rubinstein, eds. 2003. *Religion and the Formation of Taiwanese Identities*. New York: Palgrave.

Kerr, George. 1965. *Formosa Betrayed*. Boston: Houghton Mifflin Company.

Kho Kek-tun. 1996. *A History of Taiwanese Modern Development*. Taipei: Avant-garde Publishing.

Kondo, Dorinne. 1990. *Crafting Selves: Power, Gender, and Discourses of Identity in a Japanese Workplace*. Chicago: University of Chicago Press.

Lai, Tse-han, Ramon Myers, and Wei Wou. 1991. *A Tragic Beginning: The Taiwan Uprising of February 28, 1947*. Stanford: Stanford University Press.

Lee, Joseph. 1995. "Economic Development and the Evolution of Industrial Relations in Taiwan, 1950–1993." In *Employment Relations in the Growing Asian Economies*, edited by A. Verma, T. Kochan, and R. Lausburg. London: Routledge Press.

Lee, Teng-hui. 1999. *The Road to Democracy: Taiwan's Pursuit of Identity*. Tokyo: PHP Institute.

Lee, Wei-chin, and T. Y. Wang, eds. 2003. *Sayonara to the Lee Teng-hui Era: Politics in Taiwan, 1988–2000*. Lanham, Md.: University Press of America.

Lefebvre, Henri. 1991 [1974]. *The Production of Space*. Translated by Donald Nicholson-Smith. Oxford: Basil Blackwell.

Li Guozhen. 1996. "Leather Industry." *1995 Industrial Development Yearbook of the Republic of China*, pp. 624–628. Taipei: Ministry of Economic Affairs Industrial Development Bureau.

Li Ruhe, ed. 1971. *Taiwan Provincial Gazetteer*. Taipei: Historical Research Commission of Taiwan Province.

Liang Shuilan. 1986. "The Present Conditions and Hope for Development of the Taiwanese Leather Industry." *Jinri Heku* 144 (12): 84–98.

Lin, Chia-lung, and Bo Tedards. 2003. "Lee Teng-hui: Transformational Leadership in Taiwan's Transition." In *Sayonara to the Lee Teng-hui Era*, edited by W. C. Lee and T. Y. Wang, pp. 25–62. Lanham, Md.: University Press of America.

Lin, Chin-ju. 2004. "The Other Woman in Your Home: Social and Racial Discourses on 'Foreign Maids' in Taiwan." In *The Minor Arts of Daily Life: Popular Culture in Taiwan*, edited by D. K. Jordan, A. D. Morris, and M. L. Moskowitz, pp. 111–128. Honolulu: University of Hawaii Press.

Lin, Mei-rong. 1989. *Anthropology and Taiwan*. Taipei: Dao Xiang Publishers.

Lin, Tsung-yi. 1998. *An Introduction to the 2–28 Tragedy in Taiwan: For World Citizens*. Taipei: Taiwan Renaissance Foundation Press.

Lu, Hsin-yi. 2002. *The Politics of Locality: Making a Nation of Communities in Taiwan*. London: Routledge Press.

Lu, Yu-Hsia. 1998. "Women and Work in Taiwanese Family Business." Paper presented at the Conference on Social Stratification and Mobility: Newly Industrializing Economies Compared, January 7–9, Taipei.

Lyons, Thomas, and Victor Nee, eds. 1994. *The Economic Transformation of South China: Reform and Development in the Post-Mao Era.* Ithaca: Cornell University East Asia Program.

Marsh, Robert M. 1996. *The Great Transformation: Social Change in Taipei, Taiwan Since the 1960s.* Armonk, N.Y.: M. E. Sharpe.

Marx, Karl. 1963. *The Eighteenth Brumaire of Louis Bonaparte.* New York: International Publishers.

_____. 1982. "Poverty of Philosophy." In *Class, Power, and Conflict,* edited by A. Giddens and D. Held. Berkeley: University of California Press.

Mendel, Douglas. 1970. *The Politics of Formosan Nationalism.* Berkeley: University of California Press.

Morris, Andrew D. 2004. "Taiwan's History: An Introduction." In *The Minor Arts of Daily Life: Popular Culture in Taiwan,* edited by D. K. Jordan, A. D. Morris, and M. L. Moskowitz, pp. 3–31. Honolulu: University of Hawaii Press.

Murray, Stephen O., and Keelung Hong. 1994. *Taiwanese Culture, Taiwanese Society: A Critical Review of Social Science Research Done on Taiwan.* Lanham, Md.: University Press of America.

National Institute for Compilation and Translation. 1993. *Society.* Taipei: Zhong Zheng Books.

Niehoff, Justin. 1987. "The Villager as Industrialist: Ideologies of Household Manufacturing in Rural Taiwan." *Modern China* 13 (3): 278–309.

Numazaki, Ichiro. 1986. "Networks of Taiwanese Big Business: A Preliminary Analysis." *Modern China* 12 (4): 487–534.

Oxfeld, Ellen. 1993. *Blood, Sweat, and Mahjong: Family and Enterprise in an Overseas Chinese Community.* Ithaca: Cornell University Press.

Philips, Steven. 1999. "Between Assimilation and Independence: Taiwanese Political Aspirations Under Nationalist Chinese Rule, 1945–1948." In *Taiwan: A New History,* edited by Murray A. Rubinstein, pp. 275–319. Armonk, N.Y.: M. E. Sharpe.

_____. 2003. *Between Assimilation and Independence: The Taiwanese Encounter Nationalist China, 1945–1950.* Stanford: Stanford University Press.

Pred, Allan. 1990. *Making Histories and Constructing Human Geographies: The Local Transformation of Practice, Power Relations, and Consciousness.* Boulder: Westview Press.

Puri, Jyoti. 2004. *Encountering Nationalism.* London: Blackwell.

ROC Central Election Commission. 2004. Tables of Election Years and Categories, http://210.69.23.140/cec/cechead.asp (last accessed November 8, 2004).

Rofel, Lisa. 1999. *Other Modernities: Gendered Yearnings in China After Socialism.* Berkeley: University of California Press.

Rubinstein, Murray A., ed. 1999. *Taiwan: A New History.* Armonk, N.Y.: M. E. Sharpe.

Said, Edward. 1978. *Orientalism.* New York: Vintage Press.

Sangren, P. Steven. 2000. *Chinese Sociologics: An Anthropological Account of the Role of Alienation in Social Reproduction.* London: Athlone Press.

Schive, Chi. 1995. *Taiwan's Economic Role in East Asia.* Washington, D.C.: Center for Strategic and International Studies.

Scott, James C. 1985. *Weapons of the Weak: Everyday Forms of Peasant Resistance.* New Haven: Yale University Press.

Shepherd, John. 1993. *Statecraft and Political Economy on the Taiwan Frontier, 1600–1800.* Stanford: Stanford University Press.

Shieh, Gwo-shyong. 1992. *"Boss" Island: The Subcontracting Network and Micro-entrepreneurship in Taiwan's Development.* New York: Peter Lang.

_____. 1997. *Labour Only: Essays on the Labor Regime in Taiwan.* Taipei: Academia Sinica Institute of Sociology.

Shivji, Issa. 1976. *Class Struggles in Tanzania.* London: Heinemann.

Simon, Denis Fred, and Michael Y. M. Kau, eds. 1992. *Taiwan: Beyond the Economic Miracle.* Armonk, N.Y.: M. E. Sharpe.

Simon, Scott. 2003a. "Contesting Formosa: Tragic Remembrance, Urban Space, and National Identity in Taipai." *Identities: Global Studies in Culture and Power* 10 (1): 109–131.

_____. 2003b. *Sweet and Sour: Life Worlds of Taipei Women Entrepreneurs.* Lanham, Md.: Rowman and Littlefield.

Skoggard, Ian. 1996. *The Indigenous Dynamic in Taiwan's Postwar Development: The Religious and Historical Roots of Entrepreneurship.* Armonk, N.Y.: M. E. Sharpe.

Spence, Jonathon. 1990. *The Search for Modern China.* New York: W. W. Norton.

Stites, Richard. 1982. "Small-Scale Industry in Yingge, Taiwan." *Modern China* 8: 247–279.

_____. 1985. "Industrial Work as an Entrepreneurial Strategy." *Modern China* 11: 227–246.

Taiwan Region Leather Tanning Association. 1989. *The Taiwan Region Leather Tanning Association: Fortieth Anniversary Special Issue.* Taipei: Taiwan Region Leather Tanning Association.

Taylor, Charles. 1989. *Sources of the Self: The Making of Modern Identity.* Cambridge: Harvard University Press.

Thompson, E. P. 1965. *The Making of the English Working Class.* New York: Vintage Press.

_____. 1978. *The Poverty of Theory and Other Essays.* New York: Monthly Review Press.

Thornton, Arland, and Hui-sheng Lin, eds. 1994. *Social Change and the Family in Taiwan.* Chicago: University of Chicago Press.

Trouillot, Michel-Rolph. 1995. *Silencing the Past: Power and the Production of History.* Boston: Beacon Press.

_____. 2003. *Global Transformations: Anthropology and the Modern World.* New York: Palgrave Macmillan.

Tsurumi, E. Patricia. 1977. *Japanese Colonial Education in Taiwan, 1895–1945.* Cambridge: Harvard University Press.

Wachman, Alan M. 1994. *Taiwan: National Identity and Democratization.* Armonk, N.Y.: M. E. Sharpe.

Wade, Robert. 1990. *Governing the Market: Economic Theory and the Role of Government in East Asian Industrialization.* Princeton: Princeton University Press.

Wang Chen-Huan. 1993. *Capital, Labour and the State Apparatus*. Taipei: Taiwan, a Radical Quarterly in Social Studies.

Wang, Fu-chang. 1998. "Ethnic Consciousness, Nationalism and Party Support: The Ethnic Politics of Taiwan in the 1990s." *Taiwanese Sociology* 2: 1–45.

Wang, Horng-luen. 2000. "Rethinking the Global and the National: Reflections on National Imaginations in Taiwan." *Theory, Culture, and Society* 17 (4): 93–117.

Weller, Robert Paul. 1999. *Alternate Civilities: Democracy and Culture in China and Taiwan*. Boulder: Westview Press.

Wills, John E., Jr. 1999. "The Seventeenth-Century Transformation: Taiwan Under the Dutch and the Cheng Regimes." In *Taiwan: A New History*, edited by M. Rubinstein, pp. 84–106. Armonk, N.Y.: M. E. Sharpe.

Wolf, Eric. 1988. *Europe and the People Without History*. Berkeley: University of California Press.

_____. 1999. *Envisioning Power: Ideologies of Dominance and Crisis*. Berkeley: University of California Press.

Wolf, Margery. 1968. *The House of Lim*. New York: Appleton Century Crofts.

_____. 1972. *Women and the Family in Rural Taiwan*. Stanford: Stanford University Press.

Wu, Nai-Teh. 1996. "Class Identity Without Class Consciousness? Working-Class Orientations in Taiwan." In *Putting Class in Its Place: Worker Identity in East Asia*, edited by E. Perry. Berkeley: Institute of East Asian Studies.

Index